instant KEYBOARD SONGBOOK

T0068882

ISBN 978-1-4584-3793-8

HAL•LEONARD®
CORPORATION

7777 W. BLUEMOUND RD. P.O. BOX 13819 MILWAUKEE, WI 53213

For all works contained herein:
Unauthorized copying, arranging, adapting, recording, Internet posting, public performance,
or other distribution of the printed music in this publication is an infringement of copyright.
Infringers are liable under the law.

E-Z Play® Today Music Notation © 1975 by HAL LEONARD CORPORATION
E-Z PLAY and EASY ELECTRONIC KEYBOARD MUSIC are registered trademarks of HAL LEONARD CORPORATION.

Visit Hal Leonard Online at
www.halleonard.com

CONTENTS

The songs in this book are carefully coordinated with the skills introduced in the *Instant Keyboard* instruction book. Refer to the column on the right to help you determine when you're ready to play each song.

ALPHABETICAL LISTING

Deep in the Heart of Texas

Regi-Sound Program: 4
Rhythm: Country Swing or Fox Trot

Words by June Hershey
Music by Don Swander

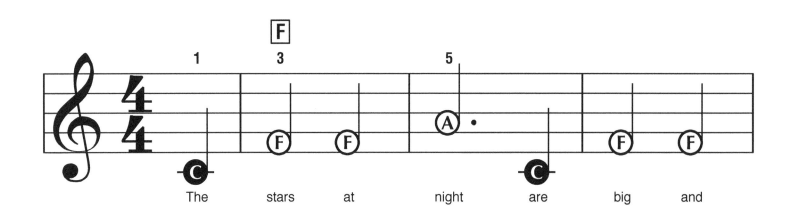

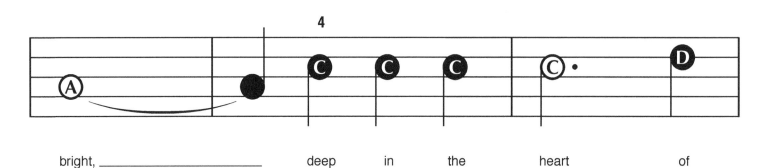

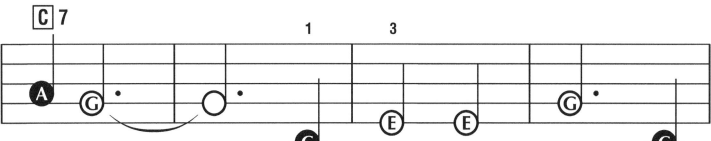

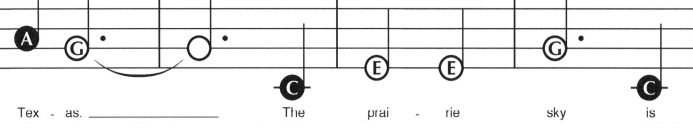

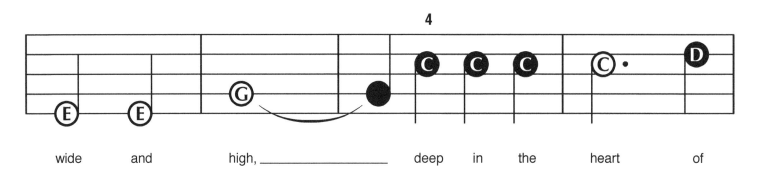

Copyright © 1941 by Melody Lane Publications, Inc.
Copyright Renewed
International Copyright Secured   All Rights Reserved

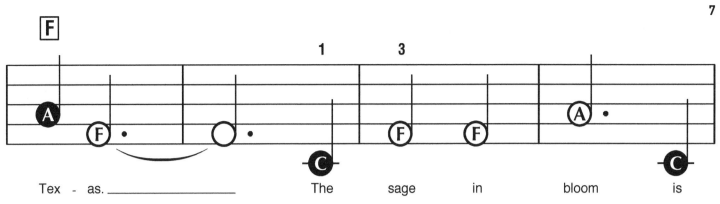

Tex - as. _____ The sage in bloom is

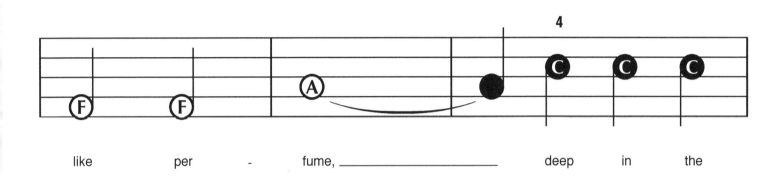

like per - fume, _____ deep in the

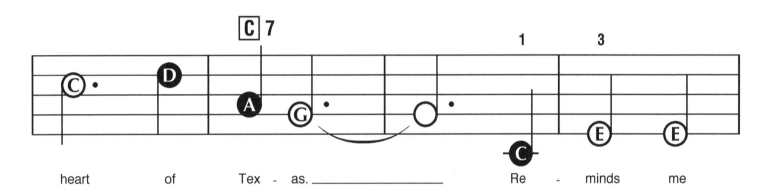

heart of Tex - as. _____ Re - minds me

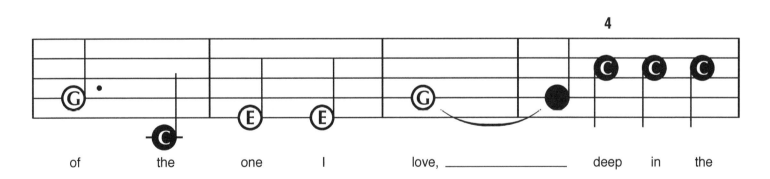

of the one I love, _____ deep in the

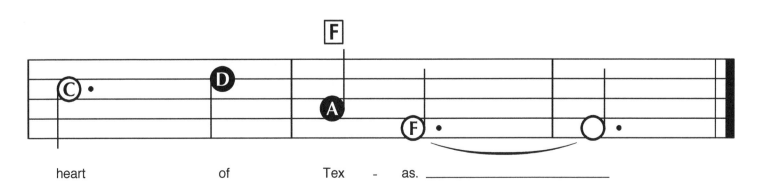

heart of Tex - as. _____

Jealous Heart

Regi-Sound Program: 7
Rhythm: Country or Fox Trot

Words and Music by
Jenny Lou Carson

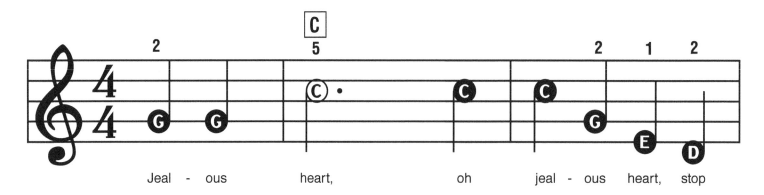

Jeal - ous   heart,   oh   jeal - ous   heart,   stop

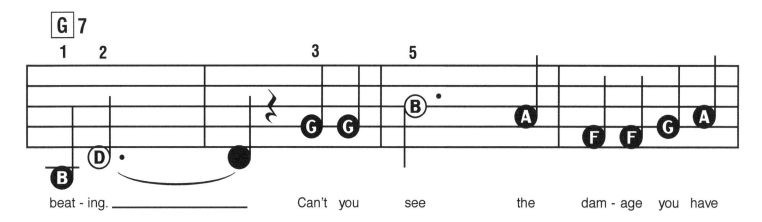

beat - ing. _____   Can't you   see   the   dam - age you have

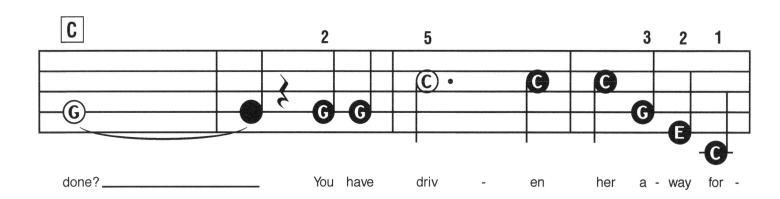

done? _____   You have   driv - en   her a - way for -

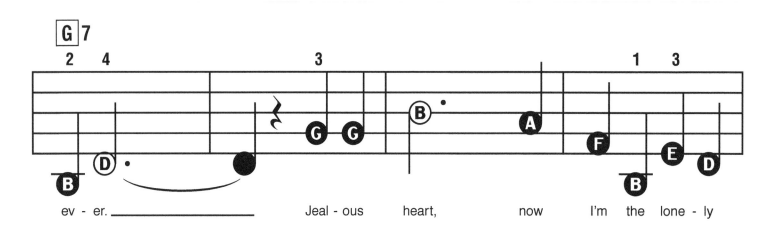

ev - er. _____   Jeal - ous   heart,   now   I'm the lone - ly

Copyright © 1944 Sony/ATV Music Publishing LLC
Copyright Renewed
All Rights Administered by Sony/ATV Music Publishing LLC, 8 Music Square West, Nashville, TN 37203
International Copyright Secured   All Rights Reserved

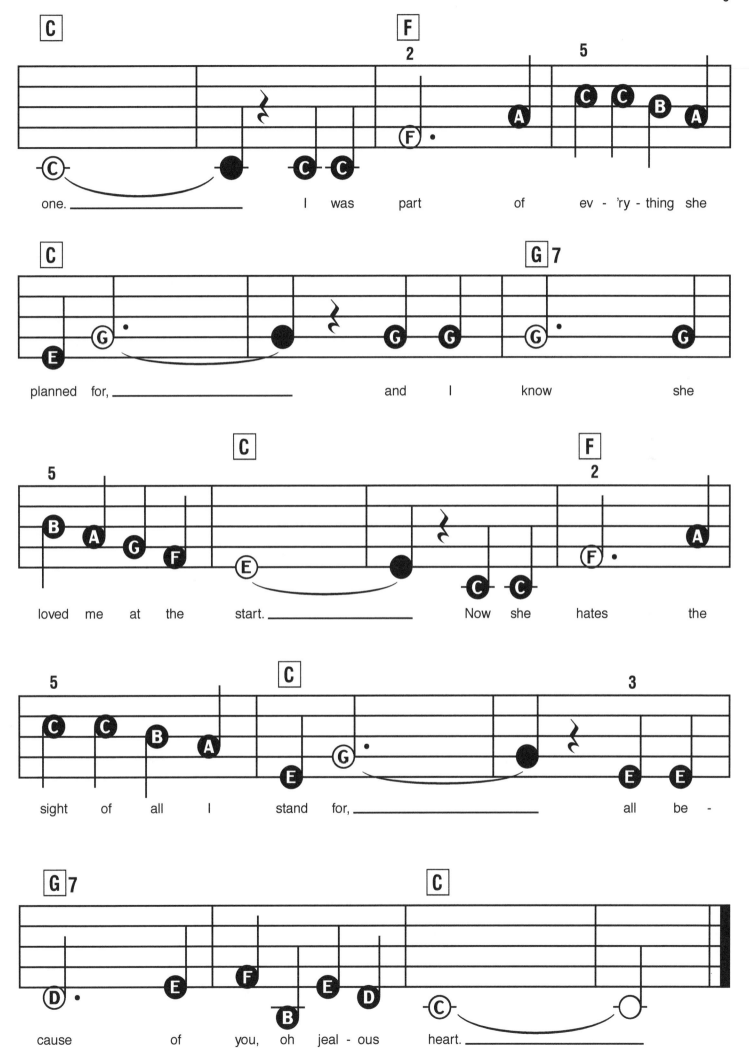

Snowbird

Regi-Sound Program: 8
Rhythm: Fox Trot or Country Swing

Words and Music by
Gene MacLellan

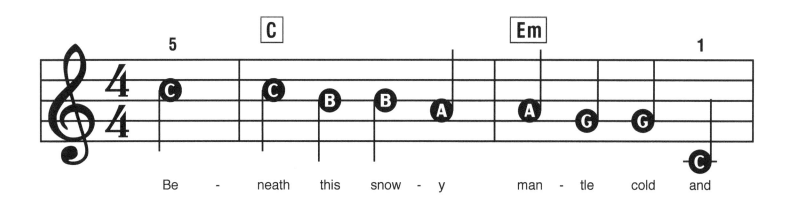

Be - neath this snow - y man - tle cold and

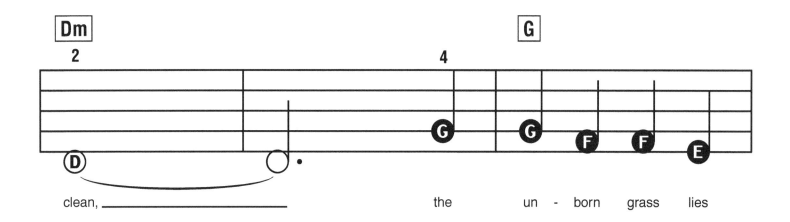

clean, _____ the un - born grass lies

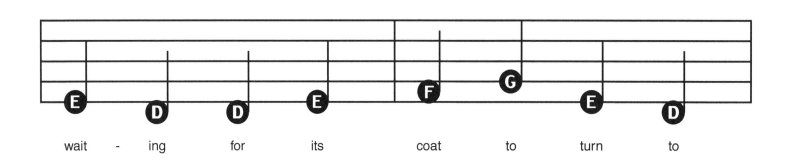

wait - ing for its coat to turn to

© 1970 (Renewed 1998) EMI BLACKWOOD MUSIC INC.
All Rights Reserved   International Copyright Secured   Used by Permission

11

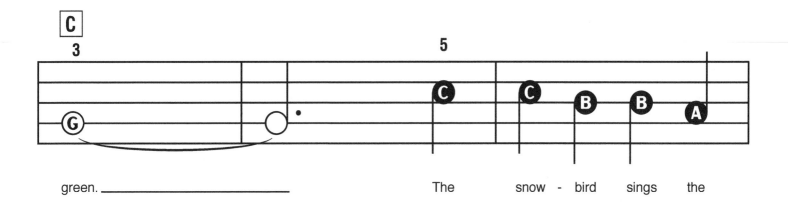

green. _____ The snow - bird sings the

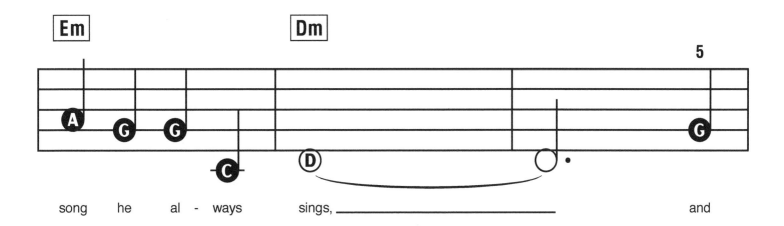

song he al - ways sings, _____ and

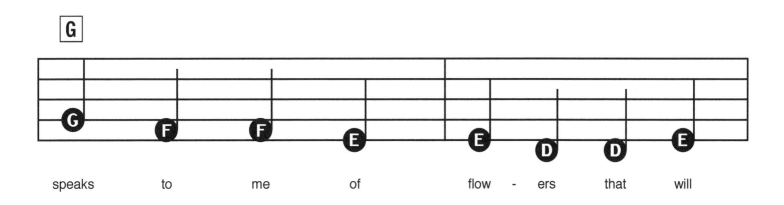

speaks to me of flow - ers that will

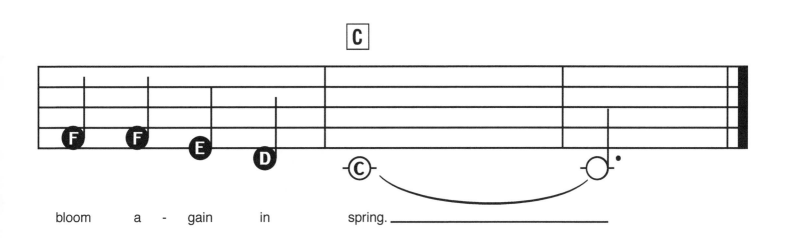

bloom a - gain in spring. _____

(Put Another Nickel In)
Music! Music! Music!

Regi-Sound Program: 8
Rhythm: Fox Trot

Words and Music by Stephan Weiss
and Bernie Baum

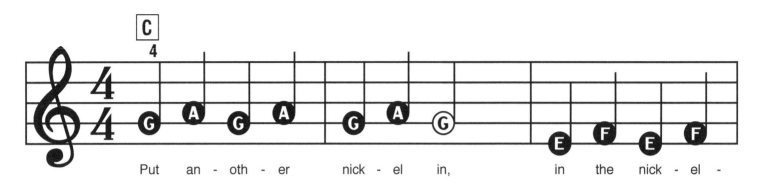

Put an - oth - er nick - el in, in the nick - el -

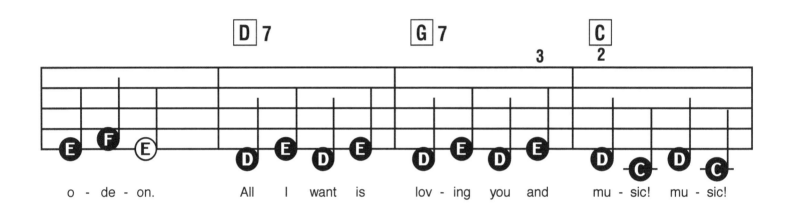

o - de - on. All I want is lov - ing you and mu - sic! mu - sic!

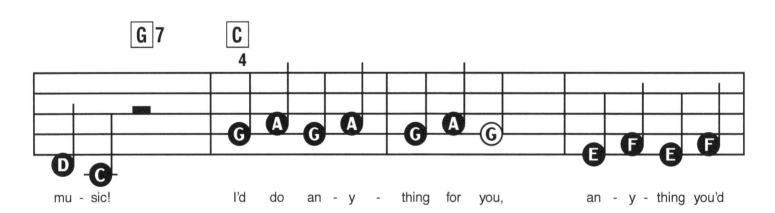

mu - sic! I'd do an - y - thing for you, an - y - thing you'd

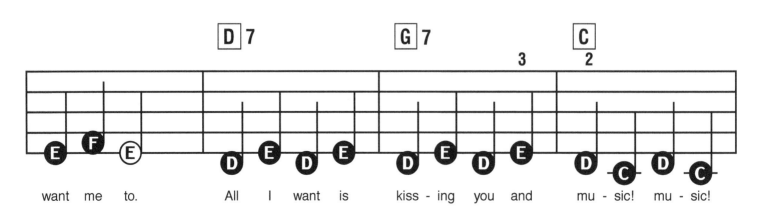

want me to. All I want is kiss - ing you and mu - sic! mu - sic!

TRO - © Copyright 1949 (Renewed) and 1950 (Renewed) Cromwell Music, Inc., New York, NY and Chappell & Co.
International Copyright Secured
All Rights Reserved Including Public Performance For Profit
Used by Permission

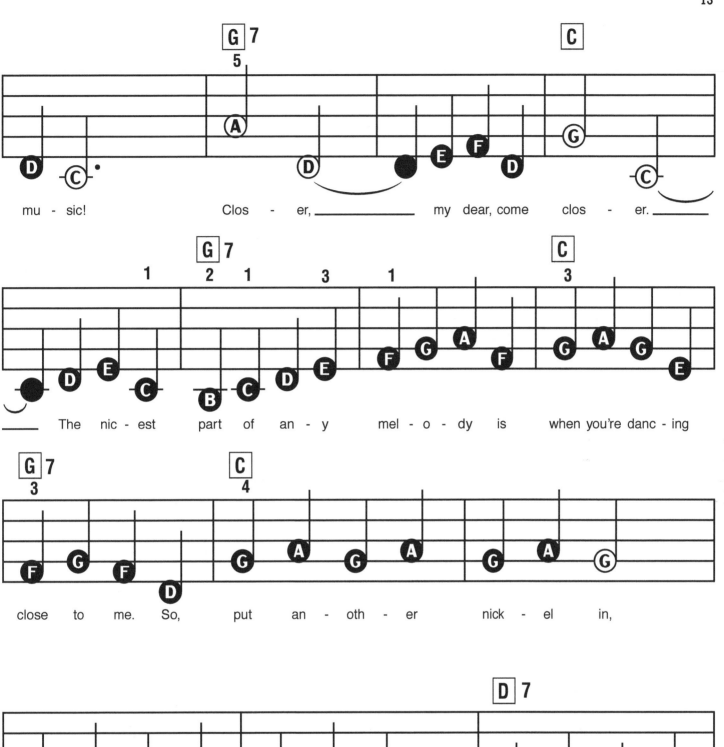

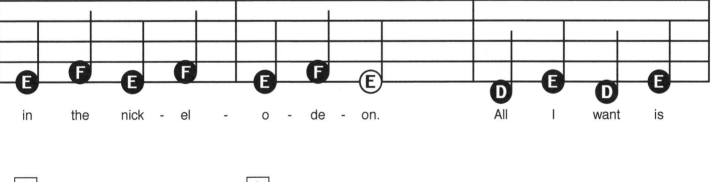

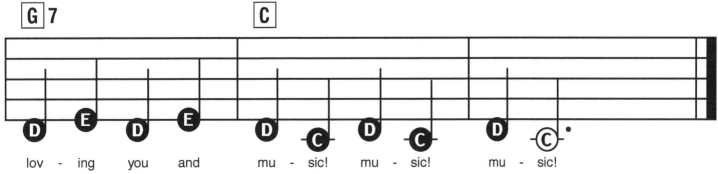

Back in the Saddle Again

Regi-Sound Program: 1
Rhythm: Country or Fox Trot

Words and Music by Gene Autry
and Ray Whitley

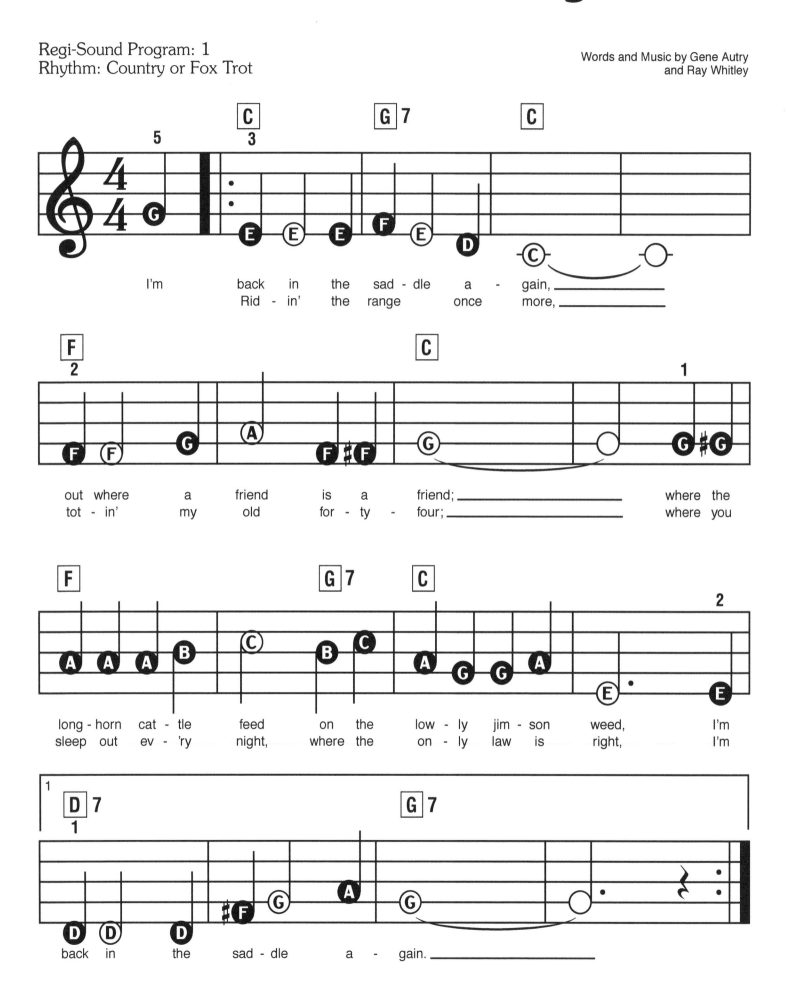

© 1939 (Renewed) Gene Autry's Western Music Publishing Co. and Katielu Music
All Rights Reserved   Used by Permission

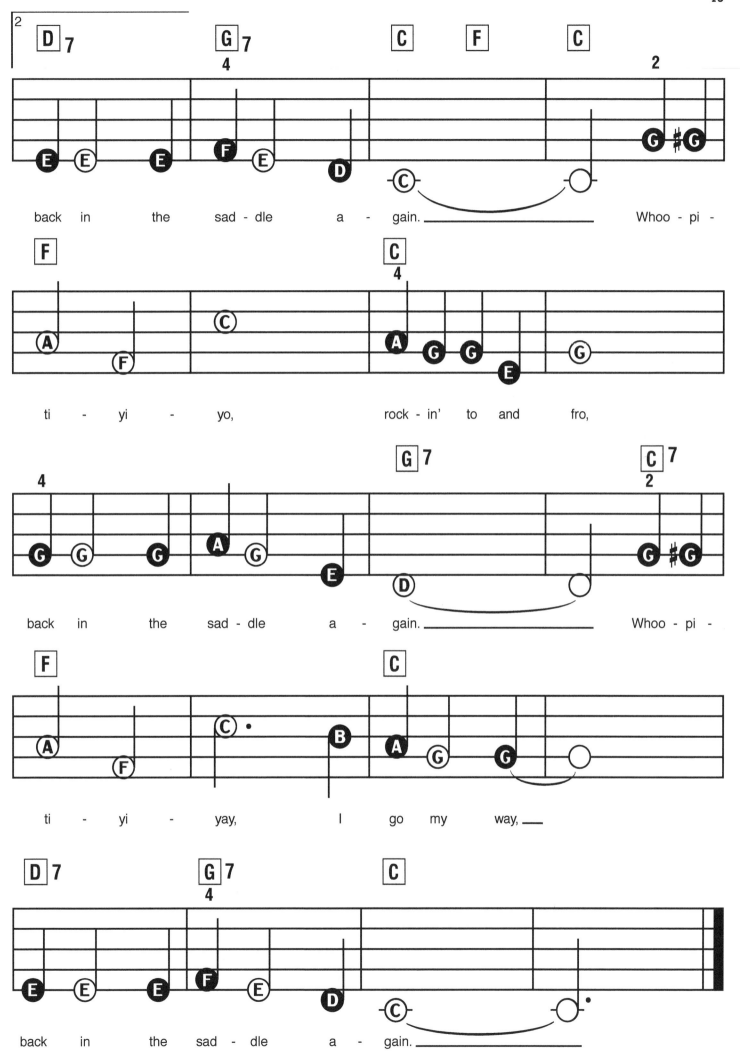

This page is intentionally left blank to eliminate a page turn.

Could I Have This Dance
from URBAN COWBOY

Regi-Sound Program: 8
Rhythm: Waltz

Words and Music by Wayland Holyfield
and Bob House

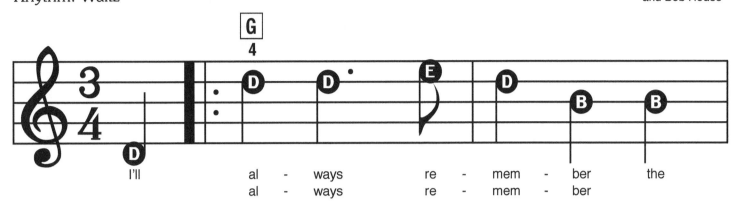

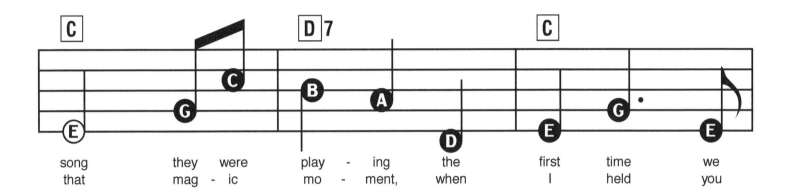

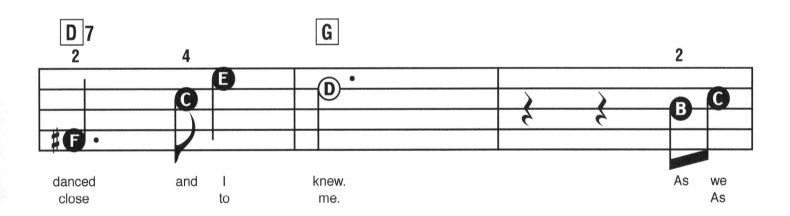

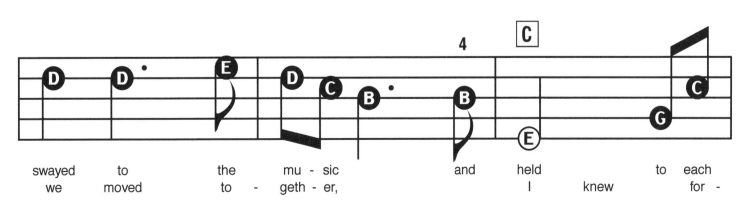

Copyright © 1980 Sony/ATV Music Publishing LLC and Universal - PolyGram International Publishing, Inc.
All Rights on behalf of Sony/ATV Music Publishing LLC Administered by Sony/ATV Music Publishing LLC,
 8 Music Square West, Nashville, TN 37203
International Copyright Secured   All Rights Reserved

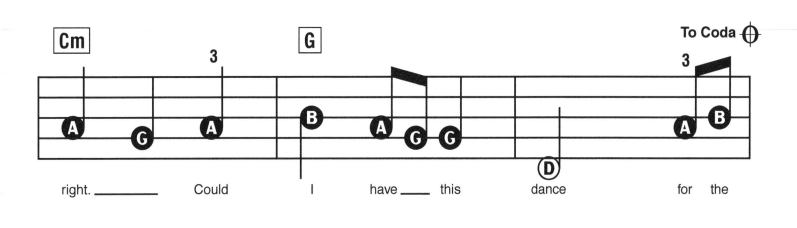

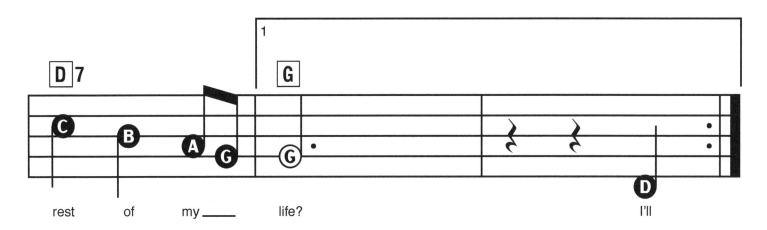

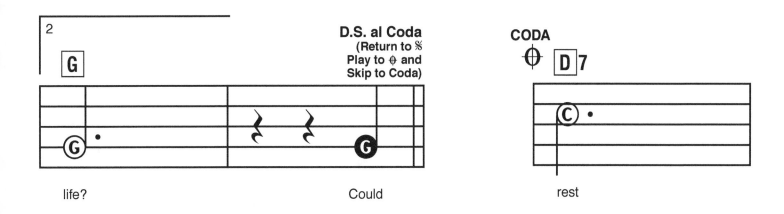

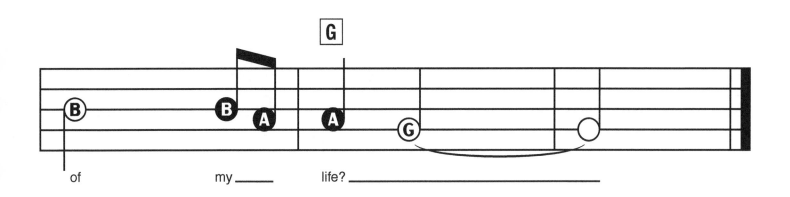

Goodnight, My Someone
from Meredith Willson's THE MUSIC MAN

Regi-Sound Program: 10
Rhythm: Waltz

By Meredith Willson

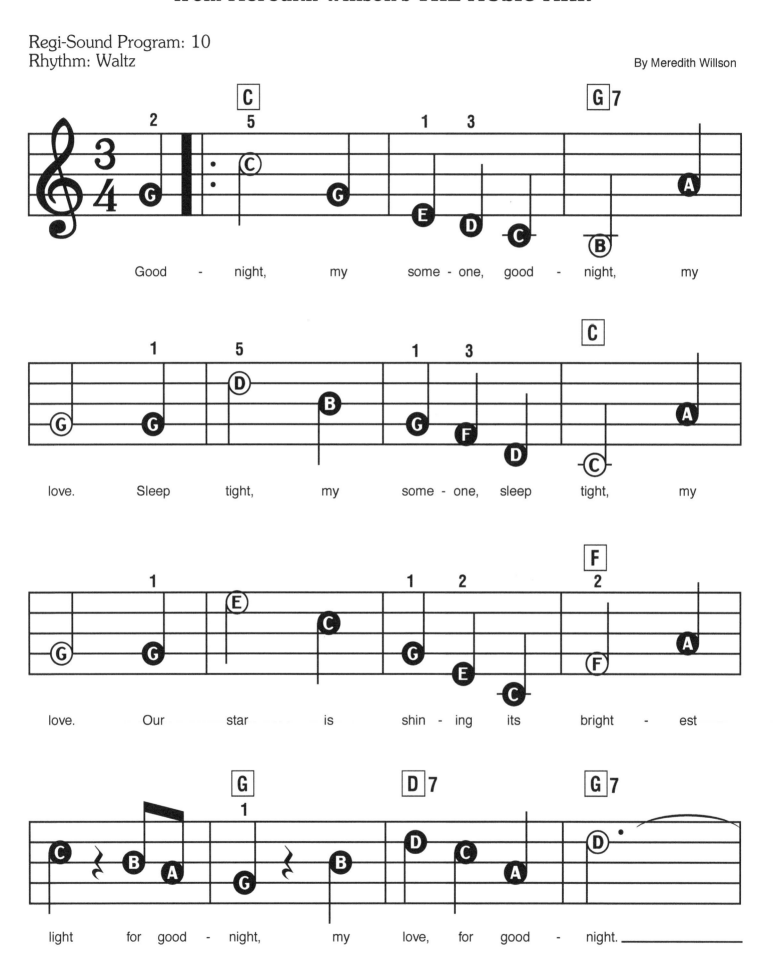

© 1957 (Renewed) FRANK MUSIC CORP. and MEREDITH WILLSON MUSIC
All Rights Reserved

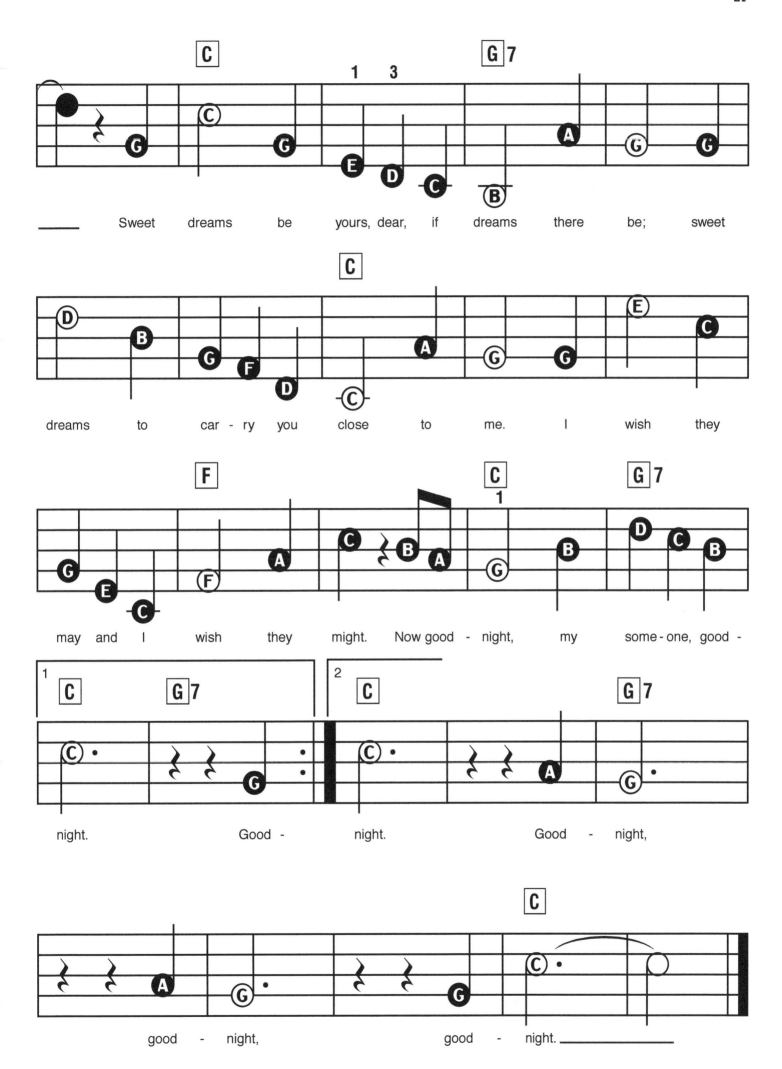

Jambalaya
(On the Bayou)

Regi-Sound Program: 4
Rhythm: Fox Trot or Country

Words and Music by
Hank Williams

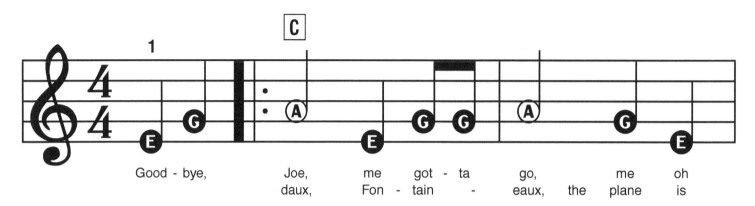

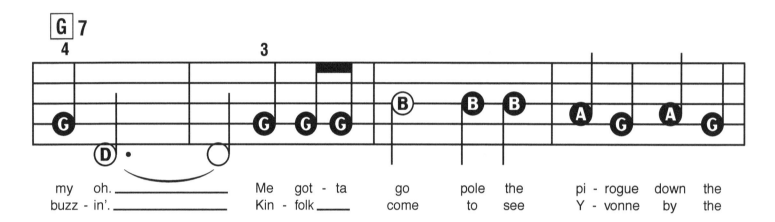

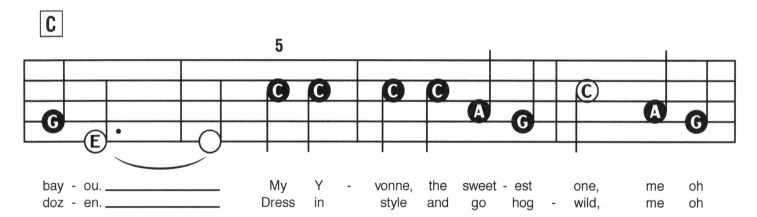

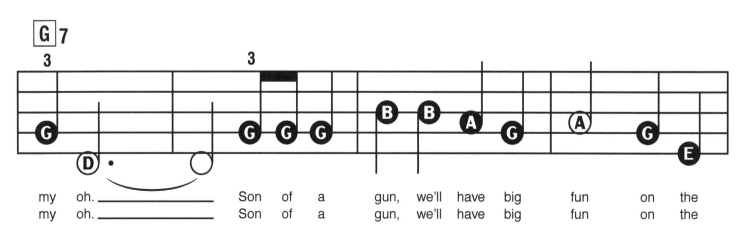

Copyright © 1952 Sony/ATV Music Publishing LLC
Copyright Renewed
All Rights Administered by Sony/ATV Music Publishing LLC, 8 Music Square West, Nashville, TN 37203
International Copyright Secured   All Rights Reserved

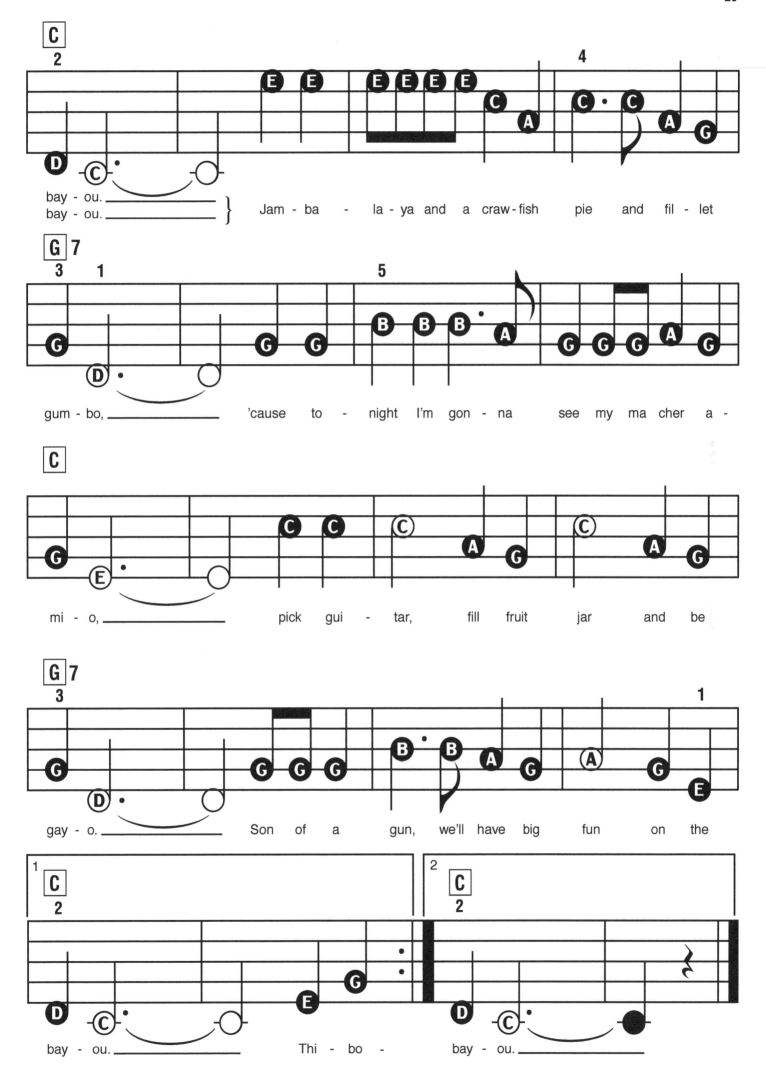

For Once in My Life

Regi-Sound Program: 1
Rhythm: Swing

Words by Ronald Miller
Music by Orlando Murden

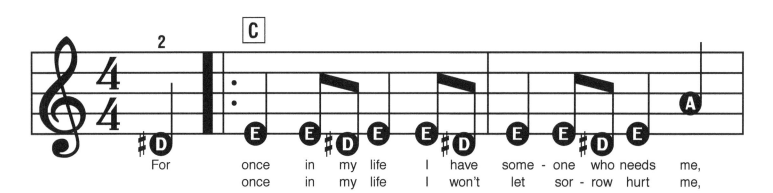

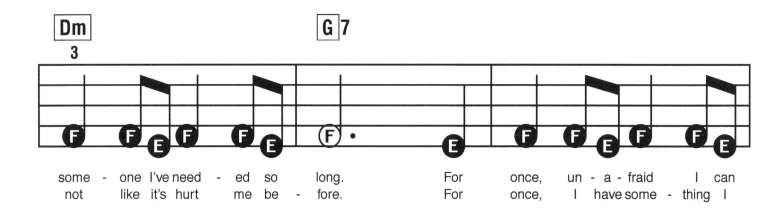

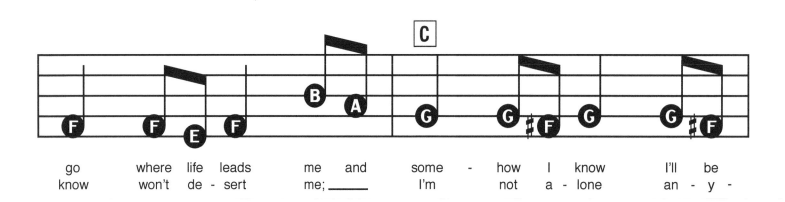

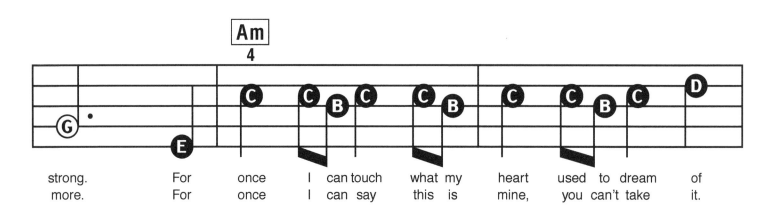

© 1965 (Renewed 1993) JOBETE MUSIC CO., INC. and STONE DIAMOND MUSIC CORP.
All Rights Controlled and Administered by EMI APRIL MUSIC INC. and EMI BLACKWOOD MUSIC INC.
All Rights Reserved   International Copyright Secured   Used by Permission

I Wish You Love

Regi-Sound Program: 8
Rhythm: Bossa Nova

English Words by Albert Beach
French Words and Music by Charles Trenet

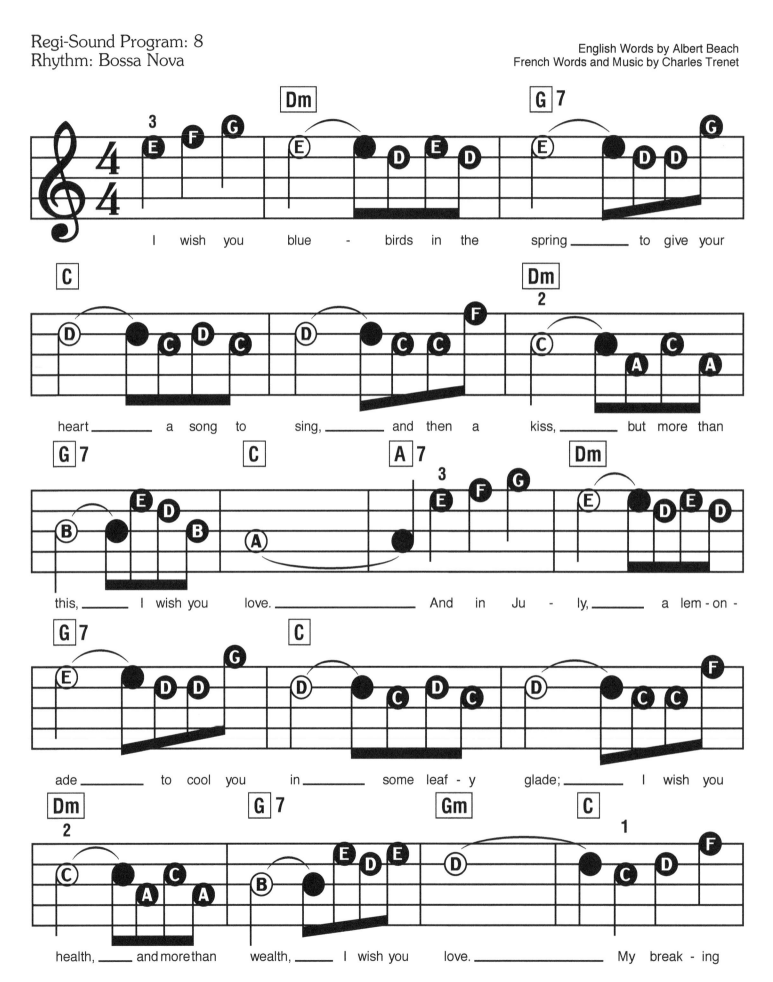

Copyright © 1946, 1955 by UNIVERSAL MUSIC - MGB SONGS and EDITIONS SALABERT
Copyright Renewed
All Rights Controlled and Administered in the USA and Canada by UNIVERSAL MUSIC CORP.
All Rights Reserved   Used by Permission

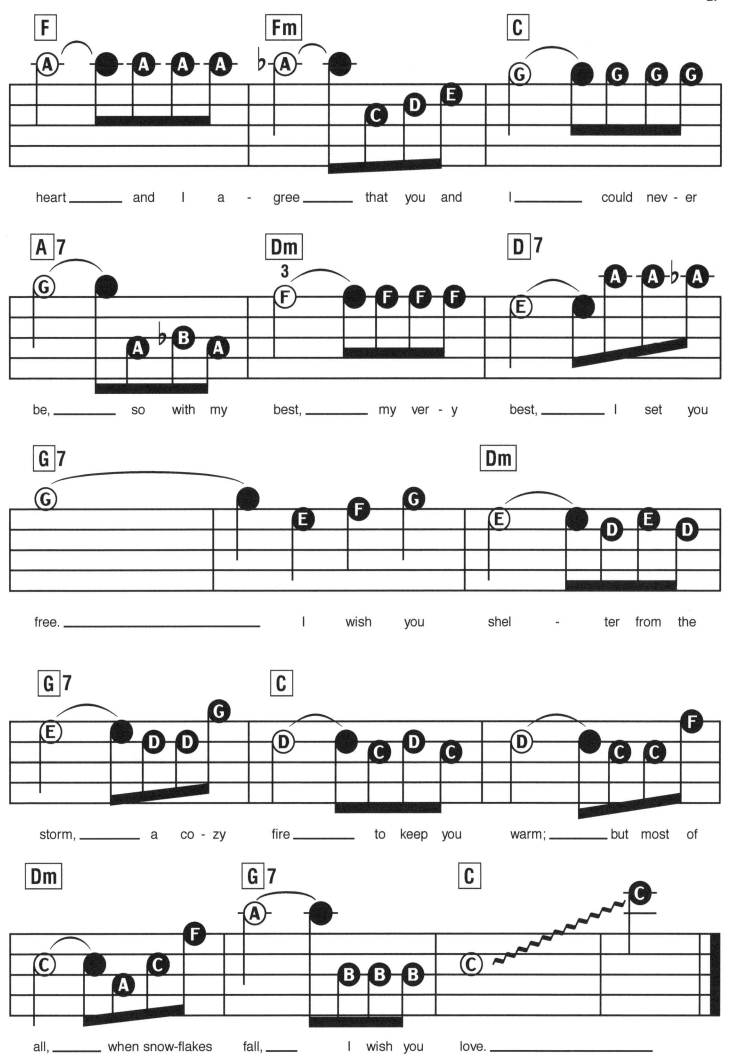

It's a Small World
from Disneyland Resort® and Magic Kingdom® Park

Regi-Sound Program: 2
Rhythm: March or Polka

Words and Music by Richard M. Sherman
and Robert B. Sherman

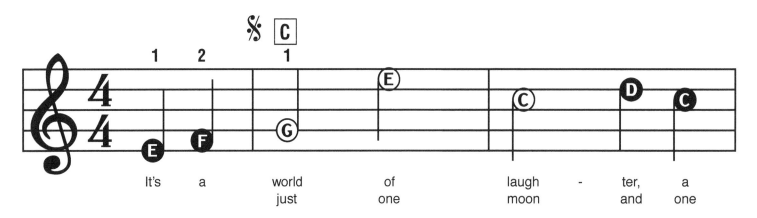

It's a world of laugh - ter, a
just one moon and one

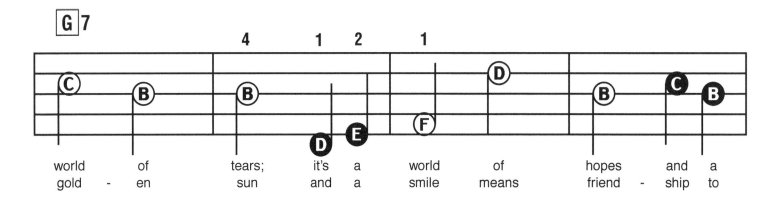

world of tears; it's a world of hopes and a
gold - en sun and a smile means friend - ship to

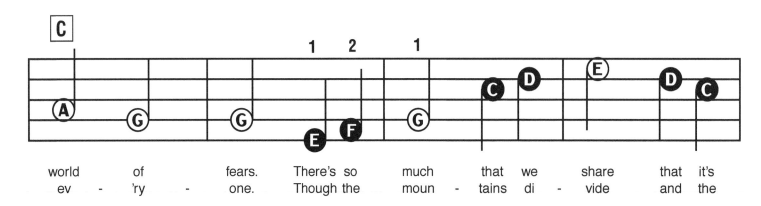

world of fears. There's so much that we share that it's
ev - 'ry - one. Though the moun - tains di - vide and the

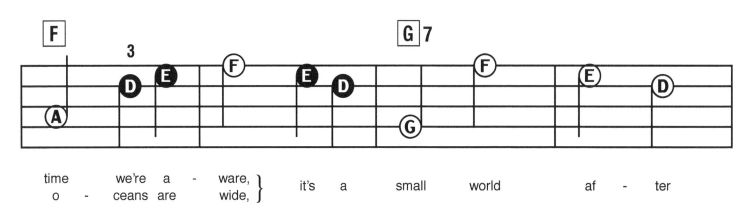

time we're a - ware,
o - ceans are wide, } it's a small world af - ter

© 1963 Wonderland Music Company, Inc.
Copyright Renewed
All Rights Reserved Used by Permission

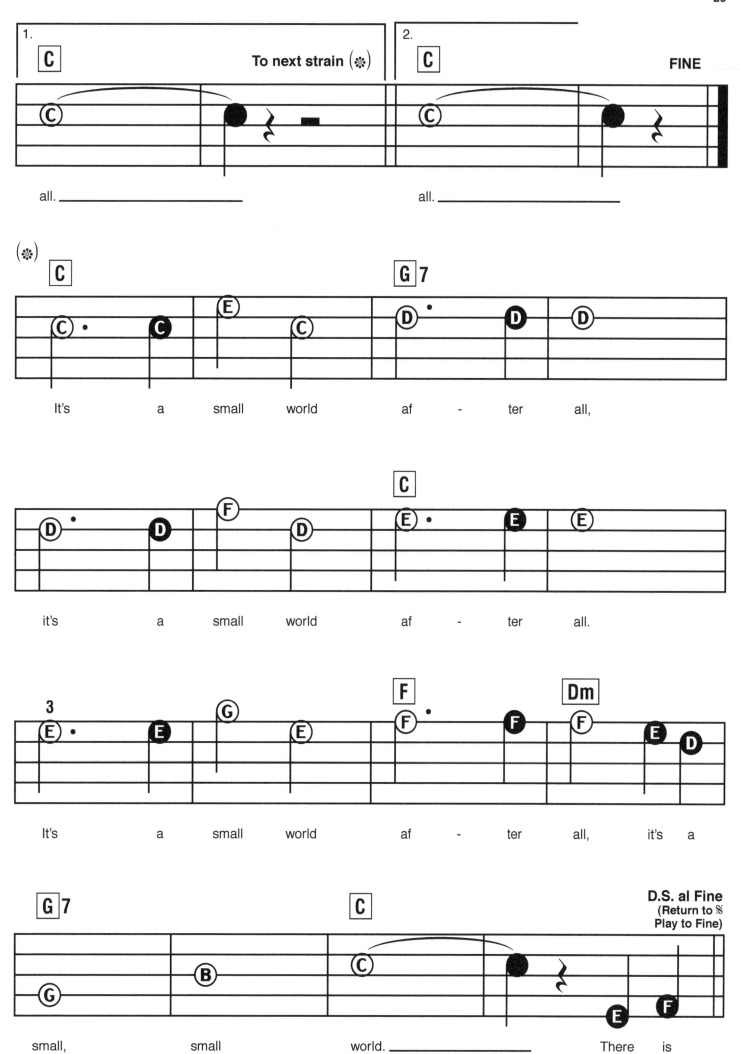

Release Me

Regi-Sound Program: 4
Rhythm: Country or Fox Trot

Words and Music by Robert Yount,
Eddie Miller and Dub Williams

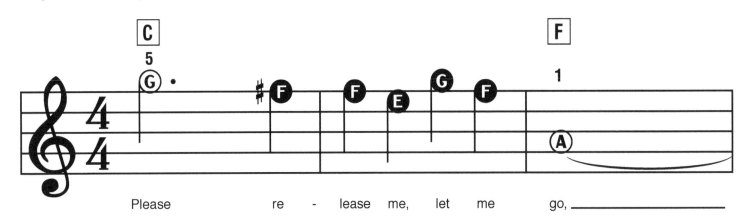

Please   re - lease me, let me   go, _____

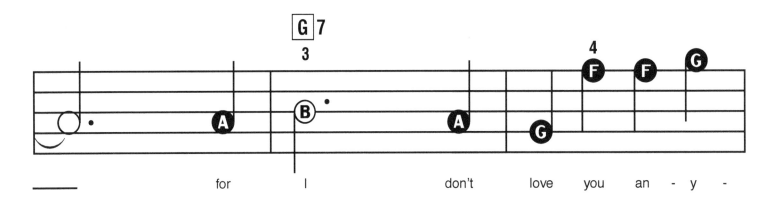

____   for   I   don't   love   you   an - y -

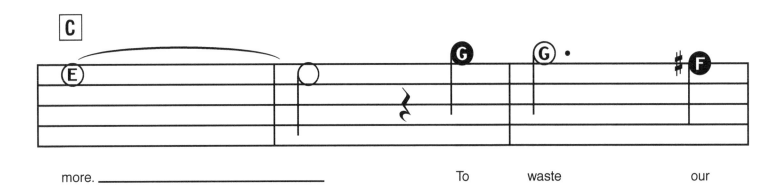

more. _____   To   waste   our

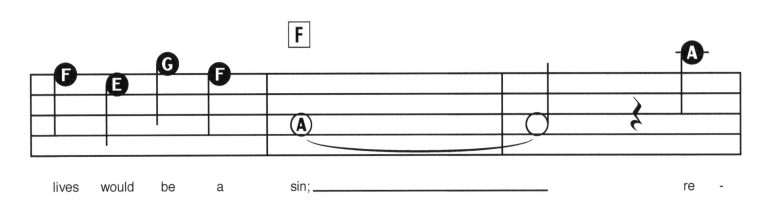

lives   would   be   a   sin; _____   re -

Copyright © 1954 Sony/ATV Music Publishing LLC and Roschelle Publishing in the U.S.A.
Copyright Renewed
All Rights outside the U.S.A. Administered by Sony/ATV Music Publishing LLC
All Rights on behalf of Sony/ATV Music Publishing LLC Administered by Sony/ATV Music Publishing Music LLC,
 8 Music Square West, Nashville, TN 37203
International Copyright Secured   All Rights Reserved

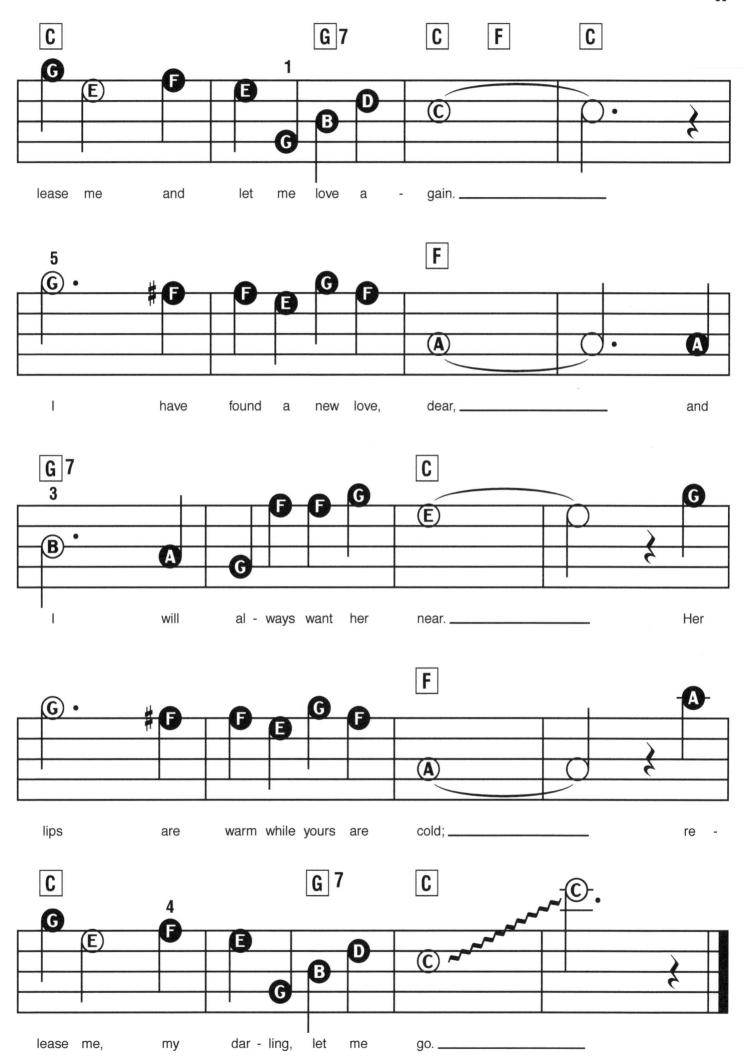

King of the Road

Regi-Sound Program: 7
Rhythm: Country or Fox Trot

Words and Music by
Roger Miller

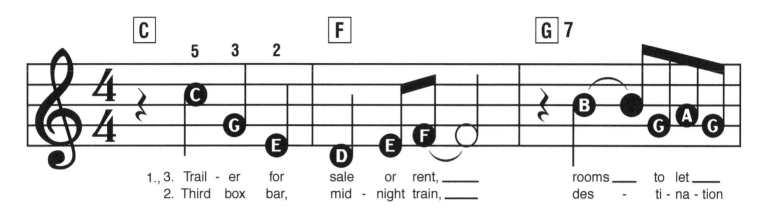

1., 3. Trail - er for sale or rent, _____ rooms _____ to let _____
2. Third box bar, mid - night train, _____ des - ti - na - tion

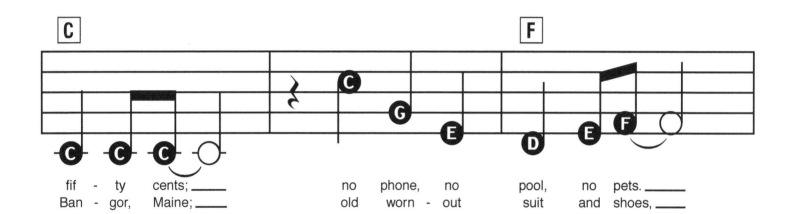

fif - ty cents; _____ no phone, no pool, no pets. _____
Ban - gor, Maine; _____ old worn - out suit and shoes, _____

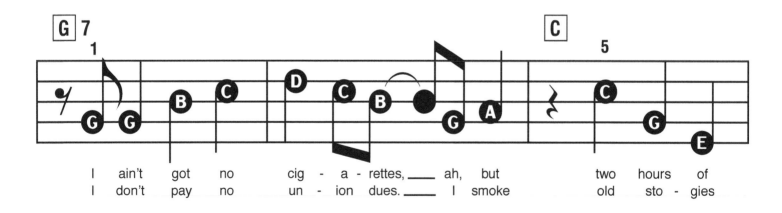

I ain't got no cig - a - rettes, _____ ah, but two hours of
I don't pay no un - ion dues. _____ I smoke old sto - gies

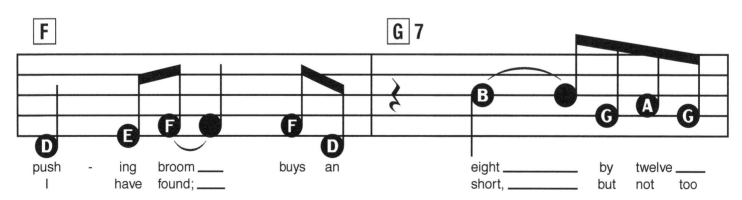

push - ing broom _____ buys an eight _____ by twelve _____
I have found; _____ short, _____ but not too

Copyright © 1964 Sony/ATV Music Publishing LLC
Copyright Renewed
All Rights Administered by Sony/ATV Music Publishing LLC, 8 Music Square West, Nashville, TN 37203
International Copyright Secured All Rights Reserved

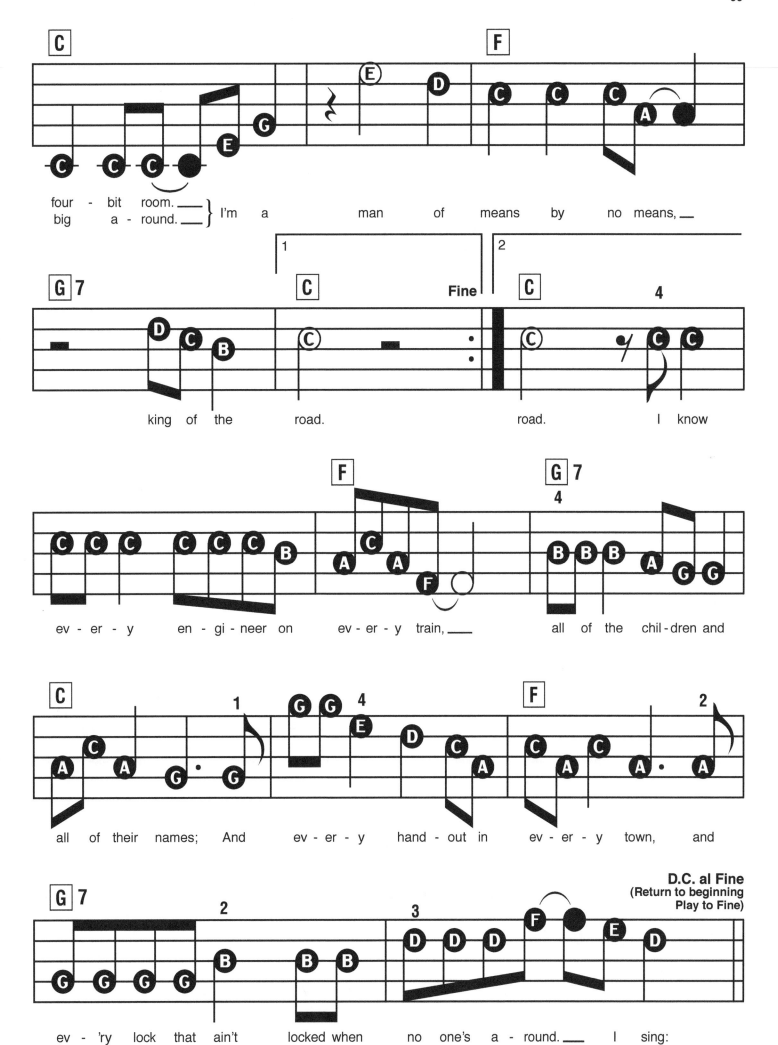

There's a Kind of Hush
(All Over the World)

Regi-Sound Program: 1
Rhythm: 8-Beat or Rock

Words and Music by Les Reed
and Geoff Stephens

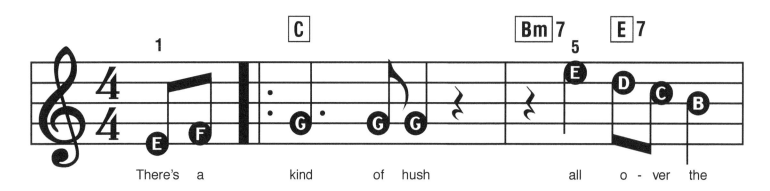

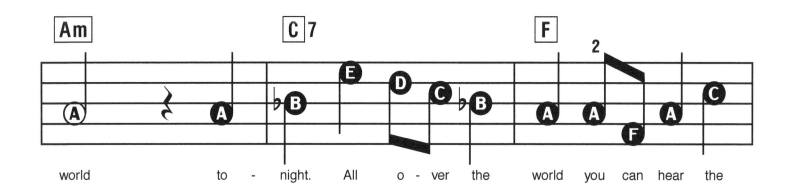

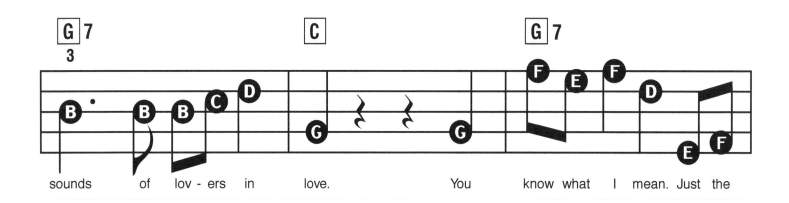

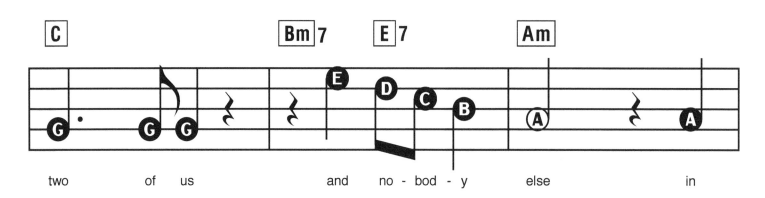

© 1966, 1967 (Renewed 1994, 1995) DONNA MUSIC, LTD. and TIC TOC MUSIC LTD.
All Rights for DONNA MUSIC, LTD. in the U.S. and Canada Controlled and Administered by GLENWOOD MUSIC CORP.
All Rights for TIC TOC MUSIC, LTD. in the U.S. and Canada Controlled and Administered by SONGS OF PEER LTD.
All Rights Reserved   International Copyright Secured   Used by Permission

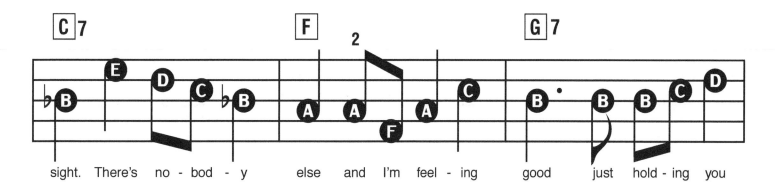

sight. There's no-bod - y   else   and I'm feel - ing   good   just hold - ing you

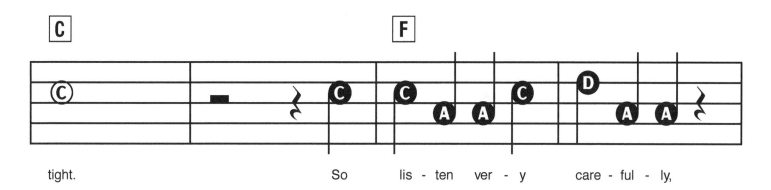

tight.   So   lis - ten ver - y   care - ful - ly,

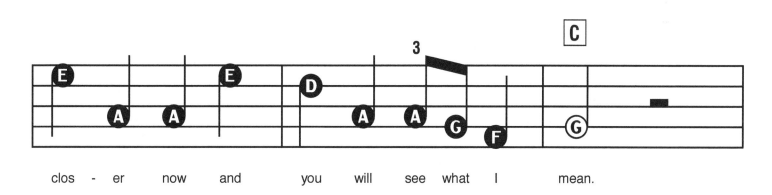

clos - er now and   you   will   see what   I   mean.

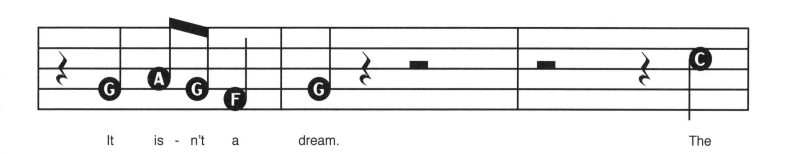

It   is - n't   a   dream.   The

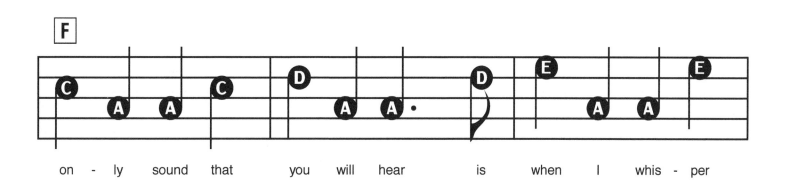

on - ly sound   that   you   will hear   is   when   I   whis - per

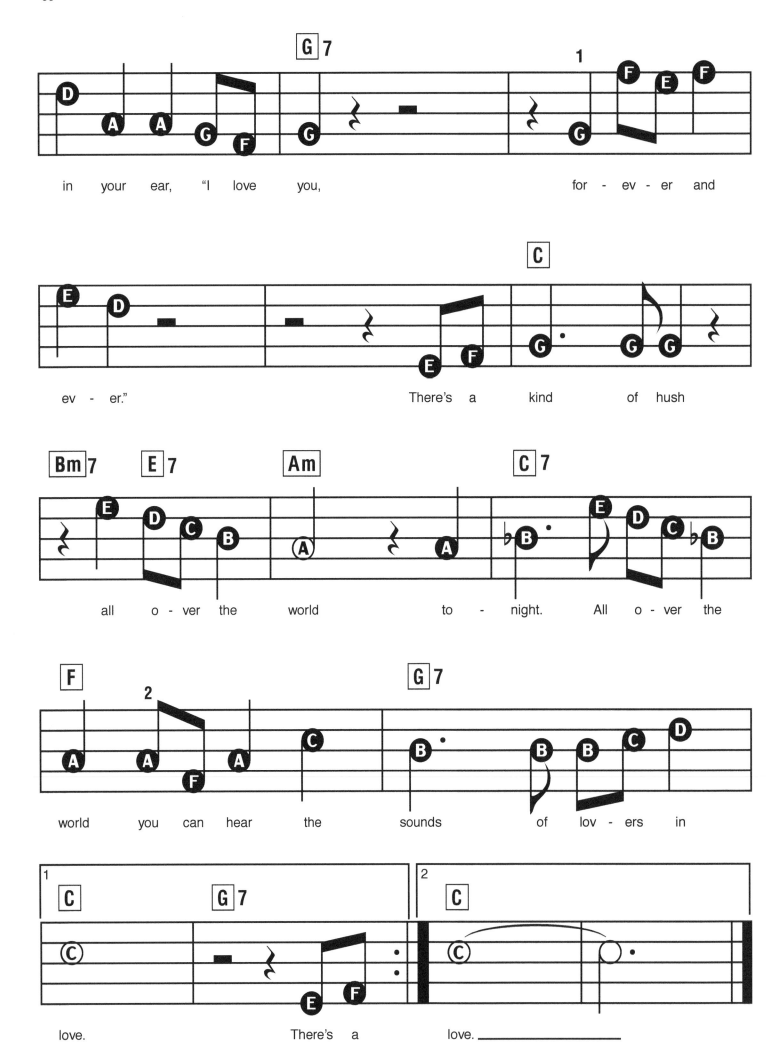

This Land Is Your Land

Regi-Sound Program: 4
Rhythm: Fox Trot or Country

Words and Music by
Woody Guthrie

Refrain

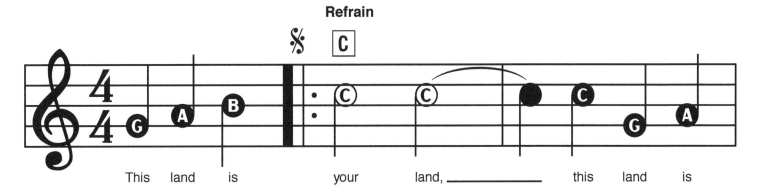

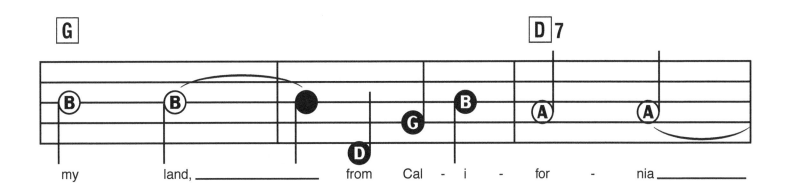

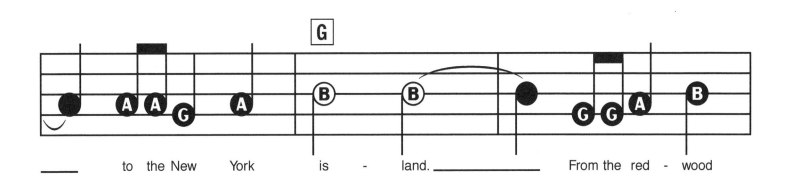

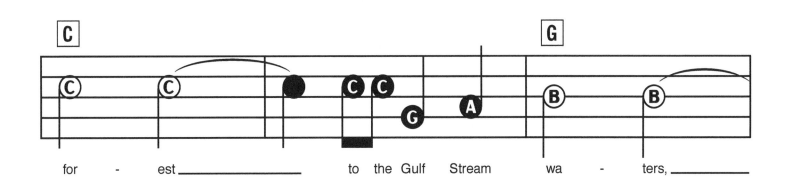

WGP/TRO - © Copyright 1956, 1958, 1970, 1972 (Copyrights Renewed) Woody Guthrie Publications, Inc.
and Ludlow Music, Inc., New York, NY
All Rights Administered by Ludlow Music, Inc.
International Copyright Secured
All Rights Reserved Including Public Performance For Profit
Used by Permission

38

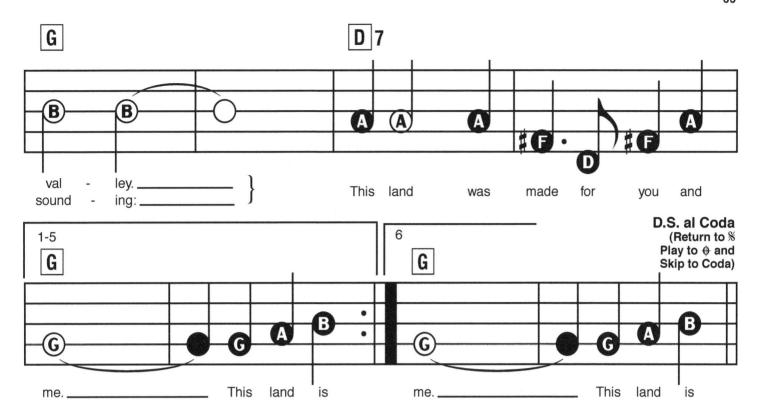

val - ley. _____
sound - ing: _____ }

This land was made for you and

me. _____ This land is   me. _____ This land is

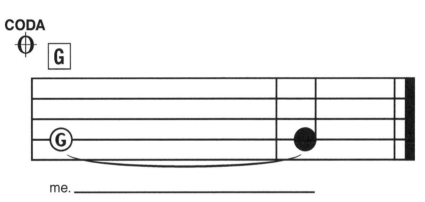

me. _____

Additional Verses

3. When the sun came shining, and I was strolling,
   And the wheat fields waving, and the dust clouds rolling,
   As the fog was lifting, a voice was chanting:
   This land was made for you and me.
   Refrain

4. As I went walking, I saw a sign there,
   And on the sign it said, "No Trespassing,"
   But on the other side it didn't say nothing;
   That side was made for you and me.
   Refrain

5. In the shadow of the steeple, I saw my people.
   By the relief office, I saw my people.
   As they stood there hungry, I stood there asking:
   Is this land made for you and me?
   Refrain

6. Nobody living can ever stop me
   As I go walking that freedom highway.
   Nobody living can ever make me turn back;
   This land was made for you and me.
   Refrain

Meditation
(Meditacão)

Regi-Sound Program: 8
Rhythm: Bossa Nova

Music by Antonio Carlos Jobim
Original Words by Newton Mendonça
English Words by Norman Gimbel

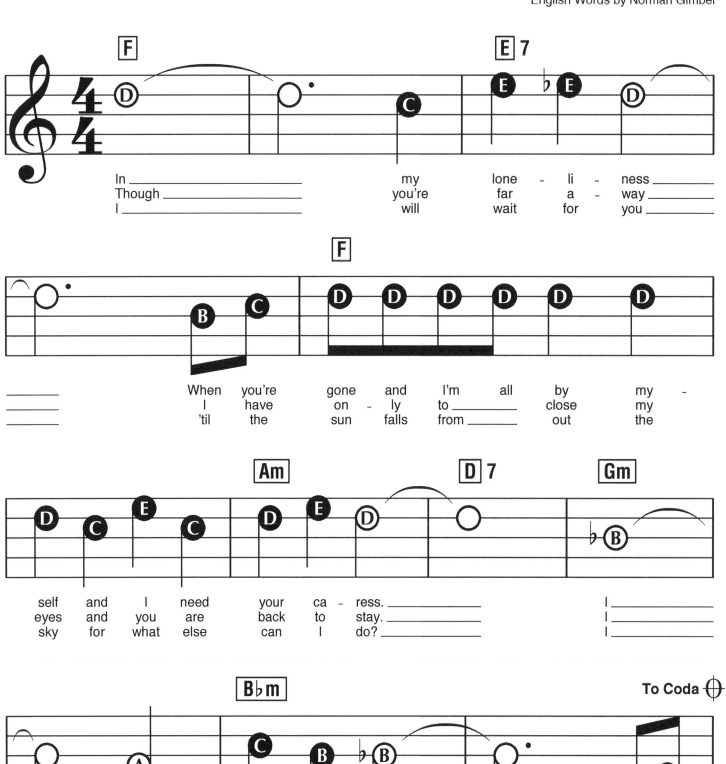

Copyright © 1963, 1964 ANTONIO CARLOS JOBIM and MRS. NEWTON MENDONCA, Brazil
Copyright Renewed and Assigned to SONGS OF UNIVERSAL, INC. and WORDS WEST LLC (P.O. Box 15187, Beverly Hills, CA 90209 USA)
All Rights Reserved   Used by Permission

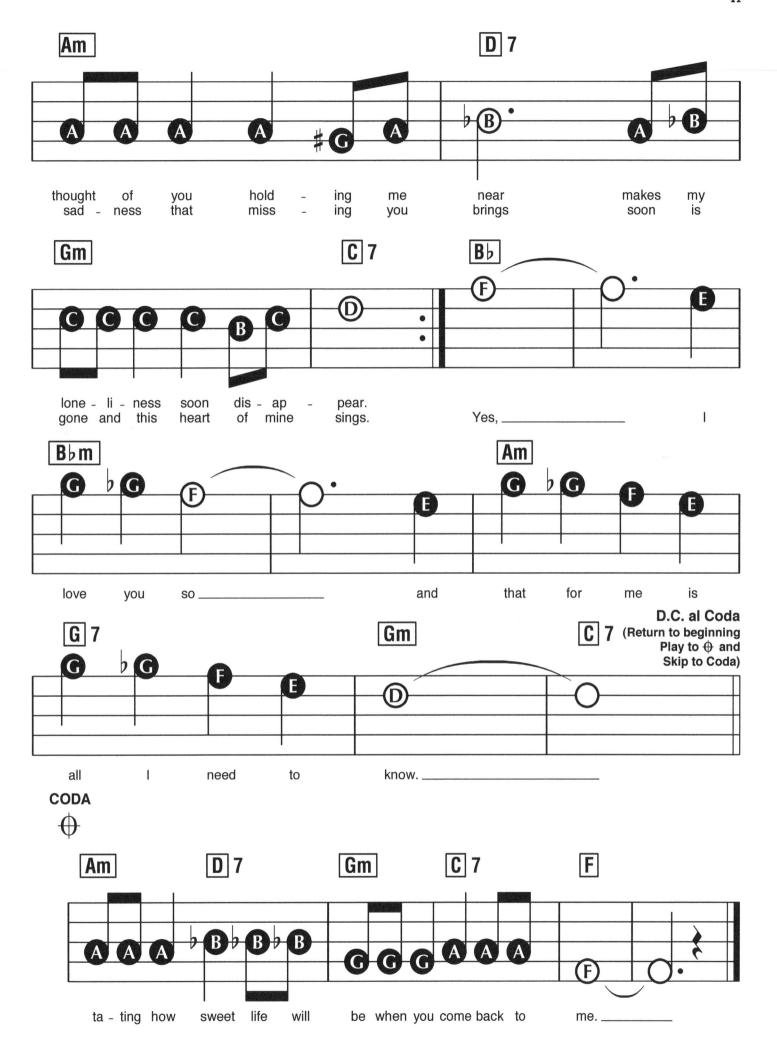

My Melody of Love

Regi-Sound Program: 2
Rhythm: Polka or March

English and Polish Lyrics by Bobby Vinton
German Lyrics by George Buschor
Music by Henry Mayer

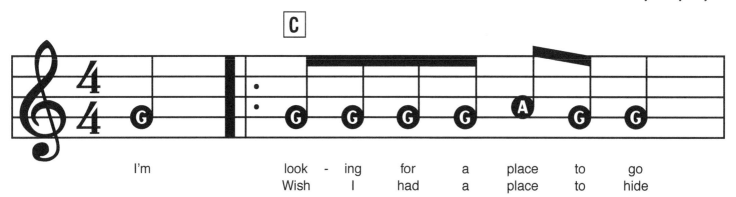

I'm look - ing for a place to go
Wish I had a place to go hide

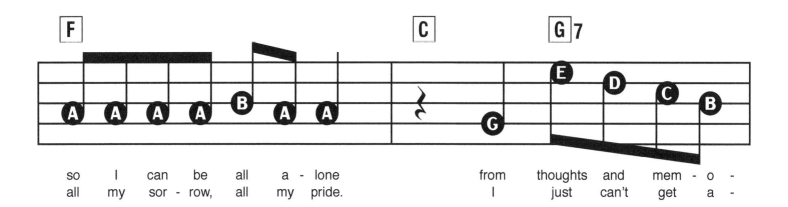

so I can be all a - lone   from thoughts and mem - o -
all my sor - row, all my pride.   I just can't get a -

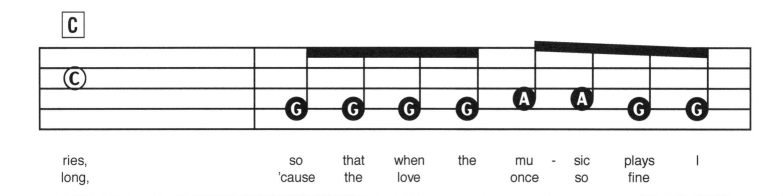

ries,   so that when the mu - sic plays I
long,   'cause the when love once so fine

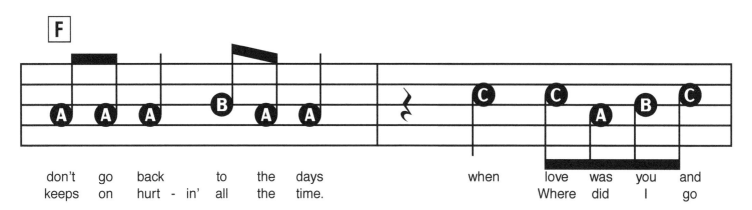

don't go back to the days   when love was you and
keeps on hurt - in' all the time.   Where did I go

Copyright © 1974 EDITION RHYTHMUS ROLF BUDDE KG, RADIO MUSIC INTERNATIONAL and GALAHAD MUSIC, INC.
Copyright Renewed
All Rights for EDITION RHYTHMUS ROLF BUDDE KG and RADIO MUSIC INTERNATIONAL Controlled
and Administered in the United States by UNIVERSAL MUSIC CORP.
All Rights Reserved Used by Permission

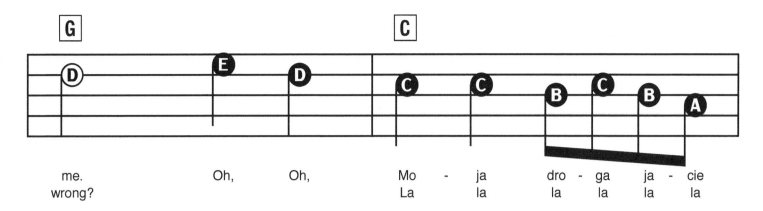

me.   Oh,   Oh,   Mo - ja   dro - ga ja - cie
wrong?   La   la   la   la   la   la

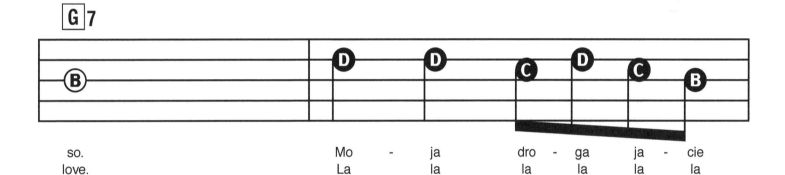

ko - cham   means that I love   you
la   la   my   mel - o - dy   of

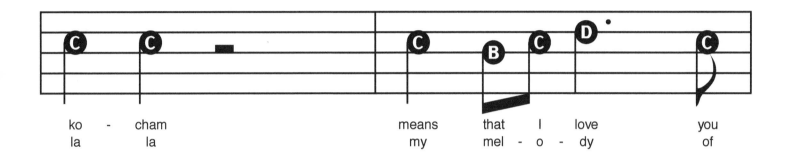

so.   Mo - ja dro - ga ja - cie
love.   La   la   la   la   la   la

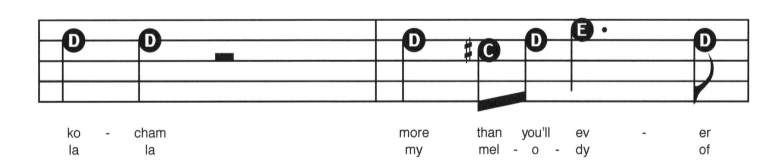

ko - cham   more than you'll ev - er
la   la   my   mel - o - dy   of

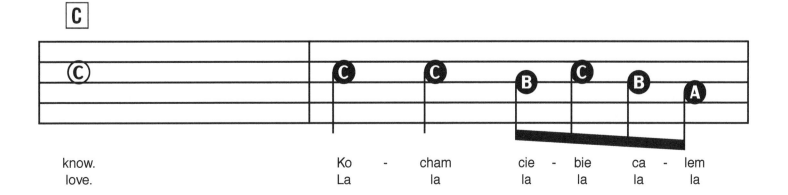

know.   Ko - cham cie - bie ca - lem
love.   La   la   la   la   la   la

44

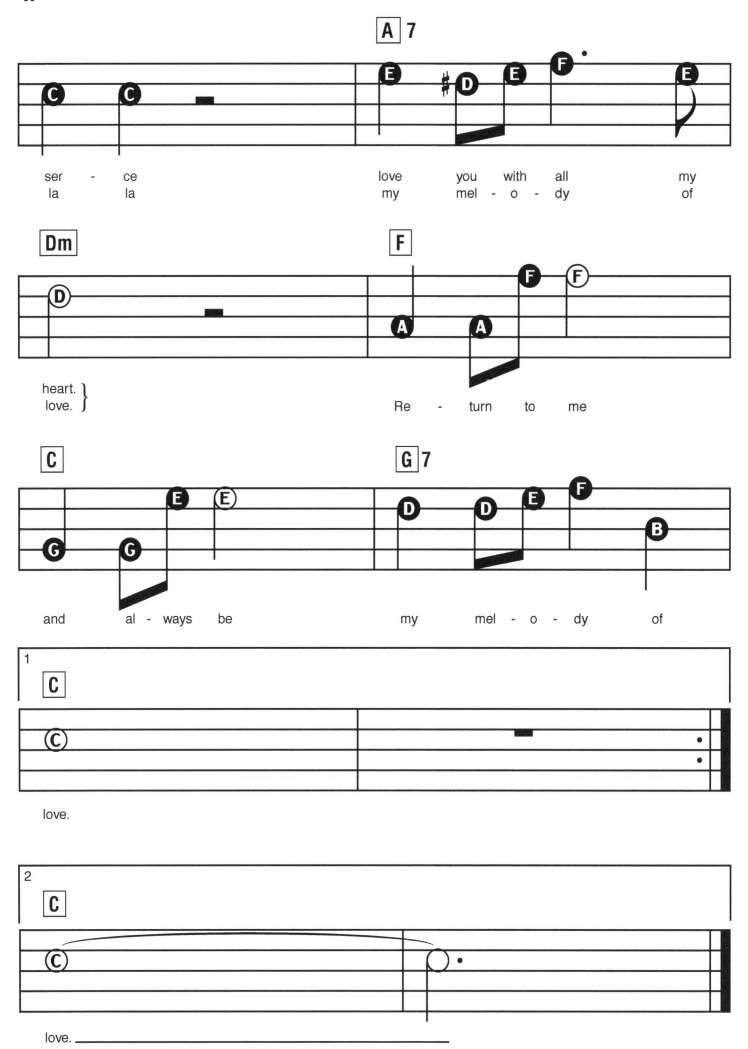

This page is intentionally left blank to eliminate a page turn.

Tic-Tock Polka

Regi-Sound Program: 7
Rhythm: Polka

Lyric by S. Guski and R.J. Martino
Music by G. Lama

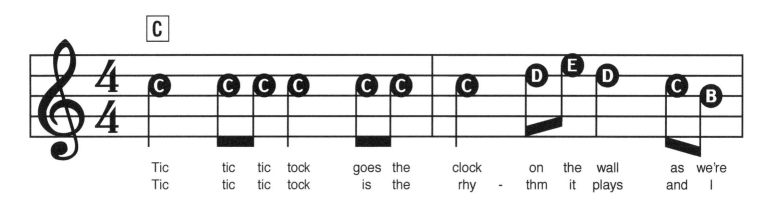

Tic   tic tic tock   goes the   clock   on the wall   as we're
Tic   tic tic tock   is the   rhy - thm it plays   and I

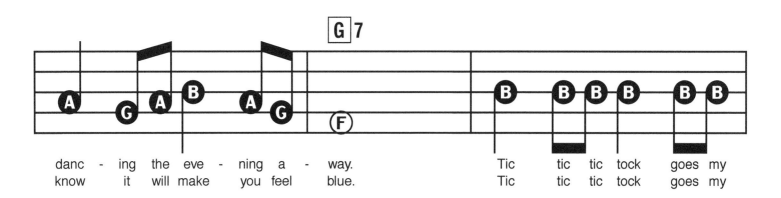

danc - ing the eve - ning a -   way.   Tic   tic tic tock   goes my
know   it will make   you feel   blue.   Tic   tic tic tock   goes my

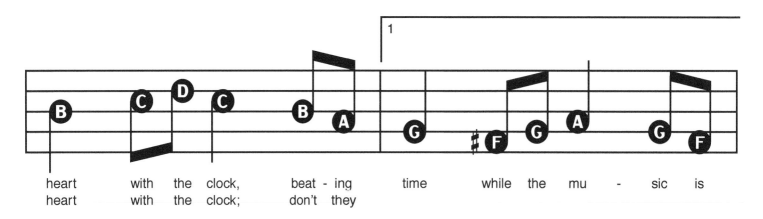

heart   with the clock,   beat - ing   time   while the mu - sic is
heart   with the clock;   don't they

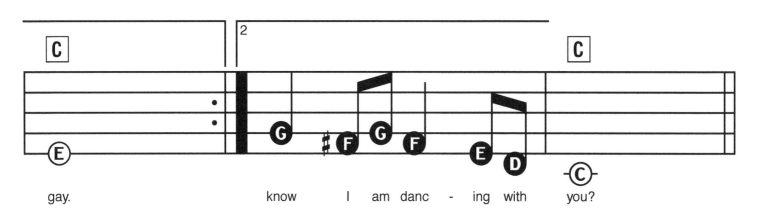

gay.   know   I am danc - ing with   you?

Copyright © 2012 by HAL LEONARD CORPORATION
International Copyright Secured All Rights Reserved

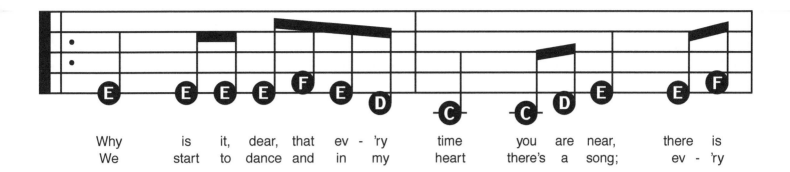

Why is it, dear, that ev - 'ry time you are near, there is
We start to dance and in my heart there's a song; ev - 'ry

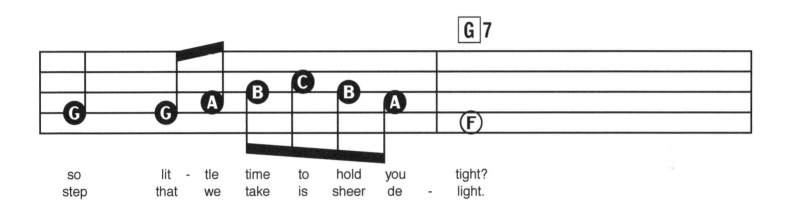

G7

so lit - tle time to hold you tight?
step that we take is sheer de - light.

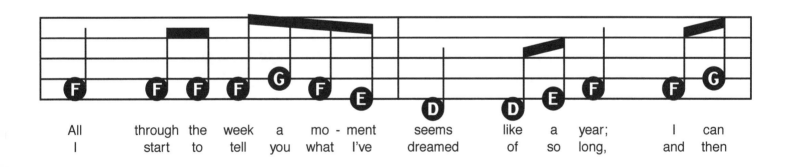

All through the week a mo - ment seems like a year; I can
I start to tell you what I've dreamed of so long, and then

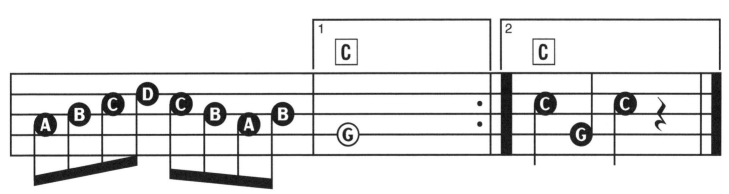

1 **C**

2 **C**

hard - ly wait un - til you come in sight.
right a - way it's time to say good - night.

I Just Called to Say I Love You

Regi-Sound Program: 2
Rhythm: 8-Beat or Rock

Words and Music by
Stevie Wonder

© 1984 JOBETE MUSIC CO., INC. and BLACK BULL MUSIC
c/o EMI APRIL MUSIC INC.
All Rights Reserved   International Copyright Secured   Used by Permission

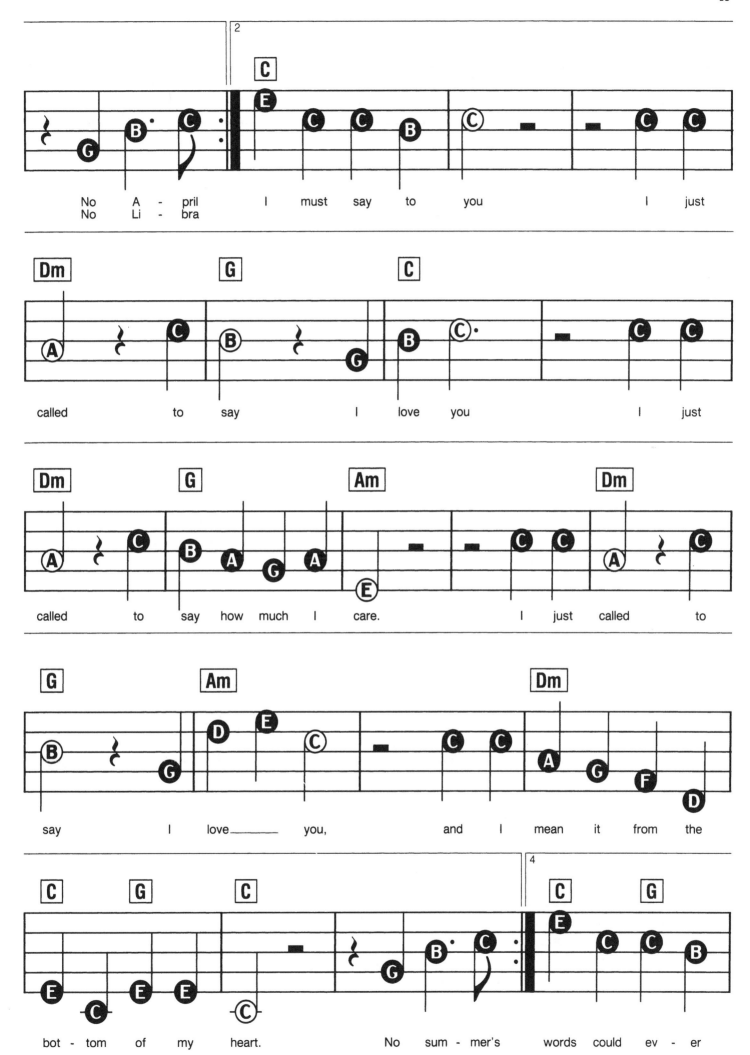

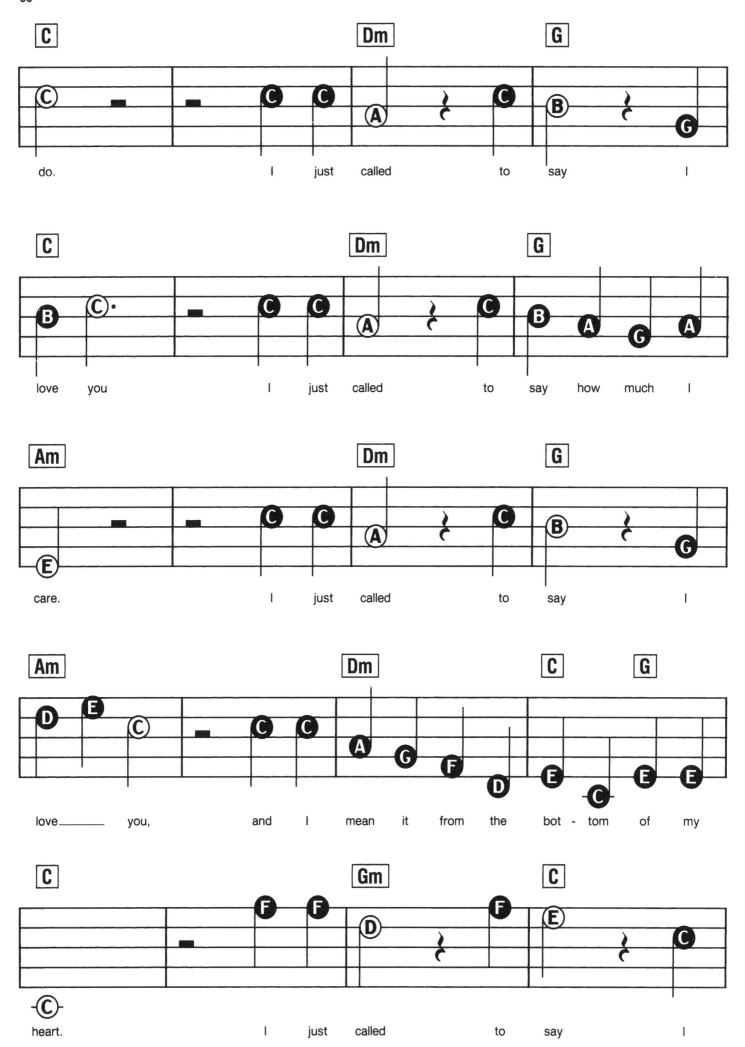

51

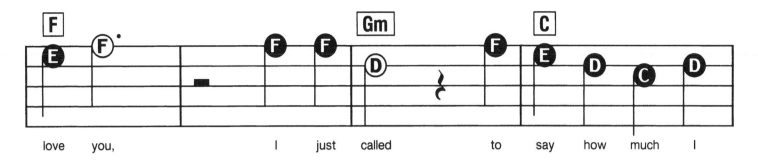

love   you,   I   just   called   to   say   how   much   I

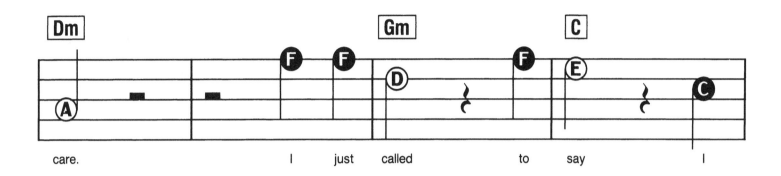

care.   I   just   called   to   say   I

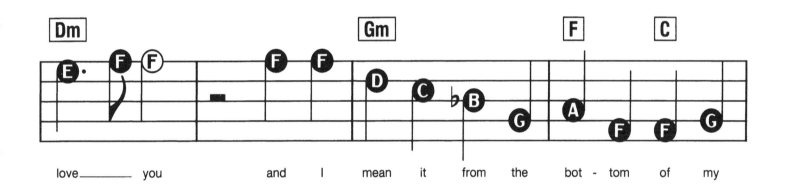

love_____ you   and   I   mean   it   from   the   bot - tom   of   my

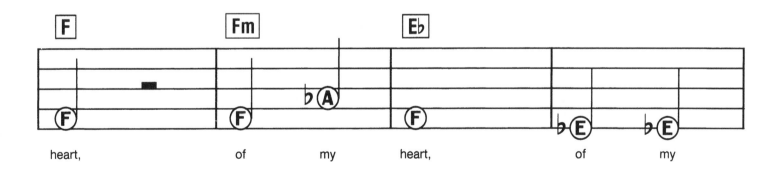

heart,   of   my   heart,   of   my

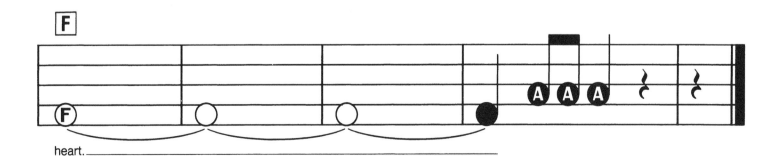

heart._____

Lady Madonna

Regi-Sound Program: 4
Rhythm: 8-Beat or Rock

Words and Music by John Lennon
and Paul McCartney

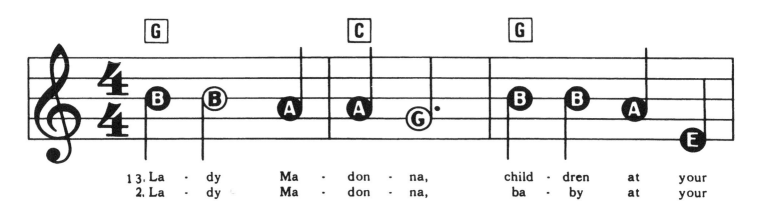

1 3. La - dy   Ma - don - na,   child - dren   at   your
2. La - dy   Ma - don - na,   ba - by   at   your

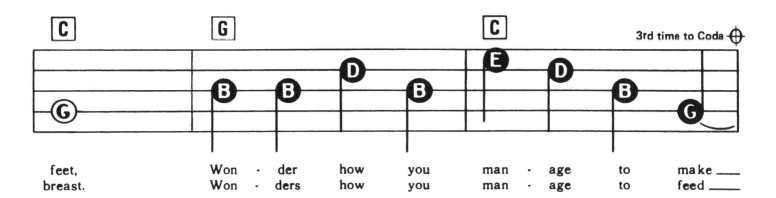

feet,   Won - der   how   you   man - age   to   make ___
breast.   Won - ders   how   you   man - age   to   feed ___

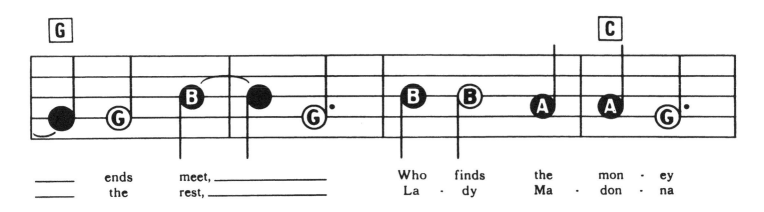

___ ends   meet, ___   Who   finds   the   mon - ey
___ the   rest, ___   La - dy   Ma - don - na

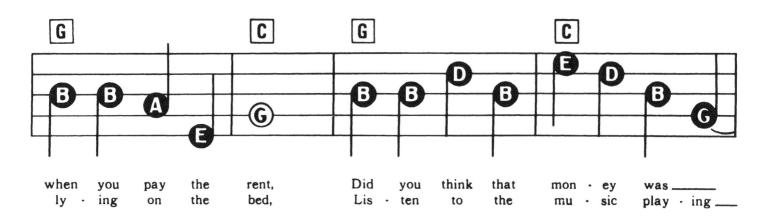

when   you   pay   the   rent,   Did   you   think   that   mon - ey   was ___
ly - ing   on   the   bed,   Lis - ten   to   the   mu - sic   play - ing ___

Copyright © 1968 Sony/ATV Music Publishing LLC
Copyright Renewed
All Rights Administered by Sony/ATV Music Publishing LLC,
  8 Music Square West, Nashville, TN 37203
International Copyright Secured   All Rights Reserved

Let It Be Me
(Je t'appartiens)

Regi-Sound Program: 8
Rhythm: 8-Beat or Rock

English Words by Mann Curtis
French Words by Pierre DeLanoe
Music by Gilbert Becaud

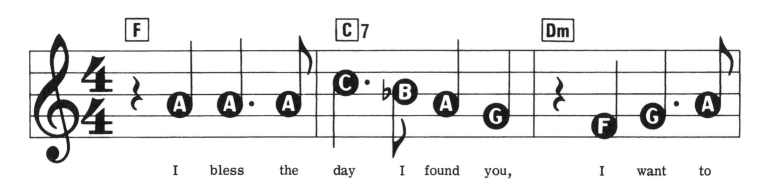

I bless the day I found you, I want to

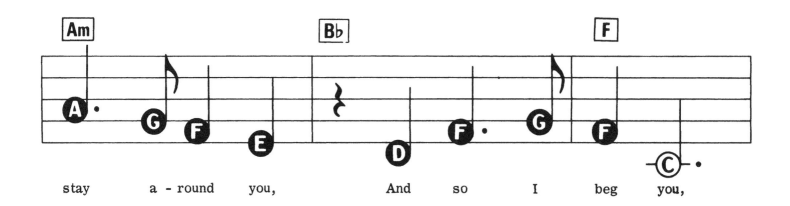

stay a - round you, And so I beg you,

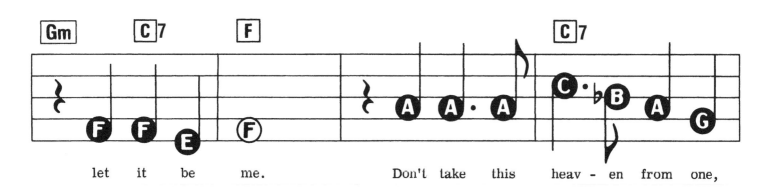

let it be me. Don't take this heav - en from one,

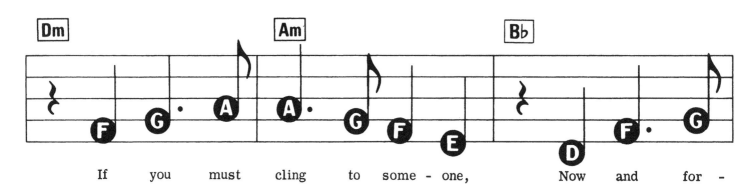

If you must cling to some - one, Now and for -

Copyright © 1955, 1957, 1960 FRANCE MUSIC COMPANY
Copyrights Renewed
All Rights for the U.S. and Canada Controlled and Administered by UNIVERSAL MUSIC CORP.
All Rights Reserved   Used by Permission

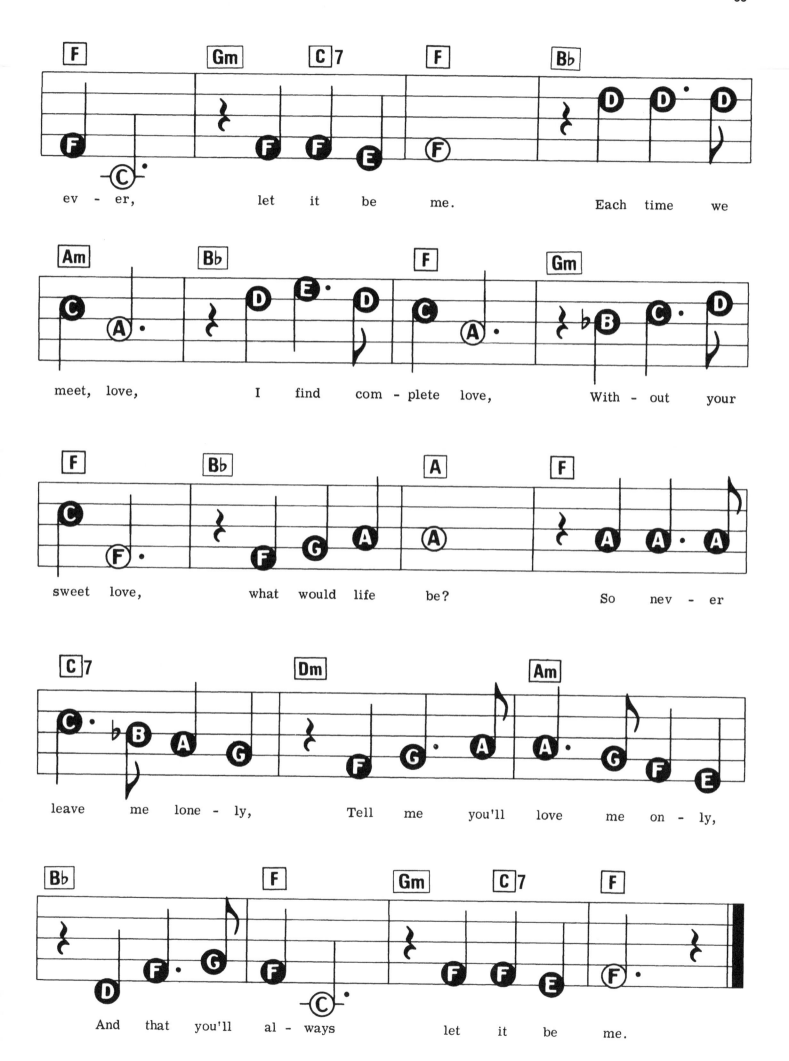

Put Your Head on My Shoulder

Regi-Sound Program: 2
Rhythm: Slow Rock or Ballad

Words and Music by
Paul Anka

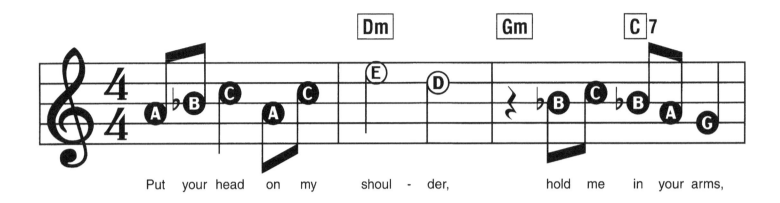

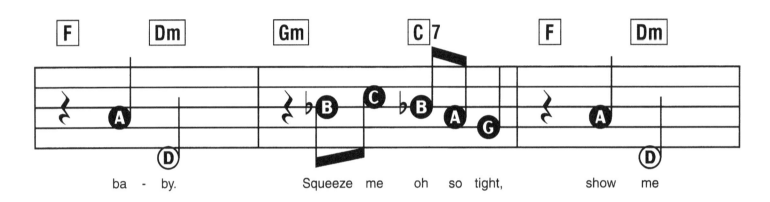

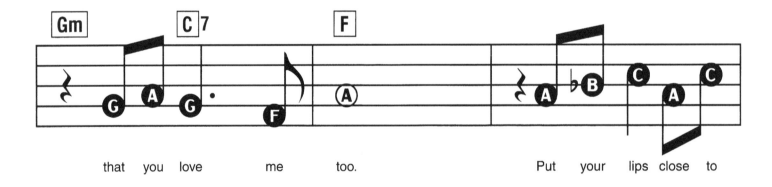

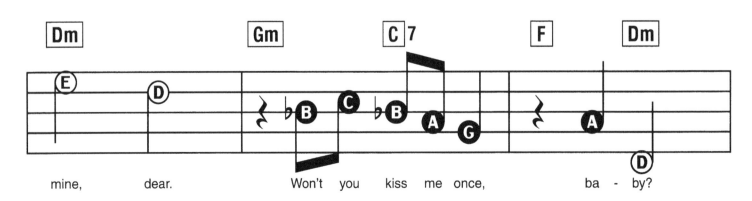

Copyright © 1958 Chrysalis Standards, Inc.
Copyright Renewed
All Rights Administered by BMG Rights Management (US) LLC
All Rights Reserved   Used by Permission

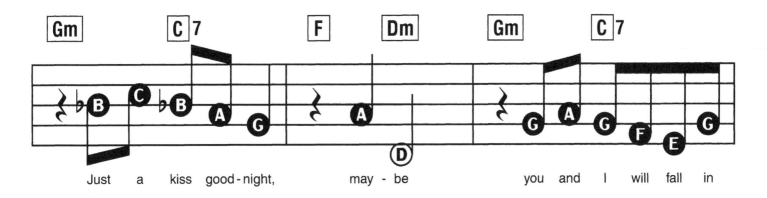

Just a kiss good-night, may-be you and I will fall in

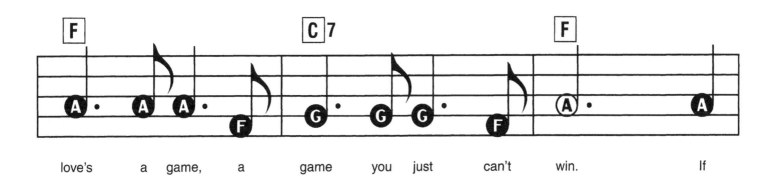

love. _____ Peo-ple say that

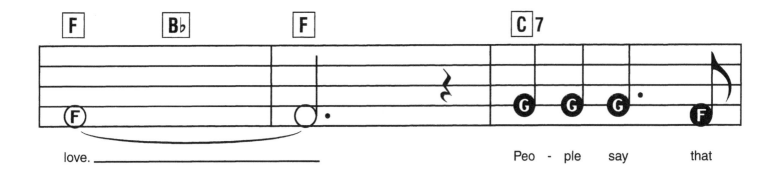

love's a game, a game you just can't win. If

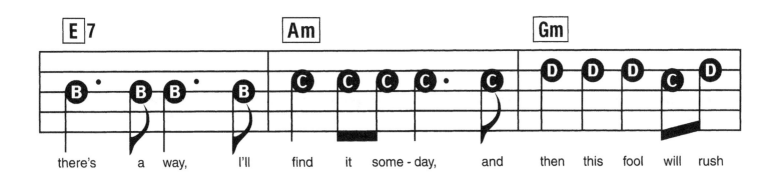

there's a way, I'll find it some-day, and then this fool will rush

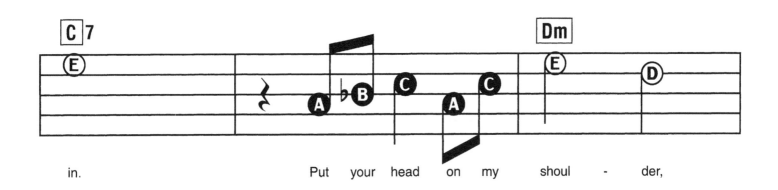

in. Put your head on my shoul-der,

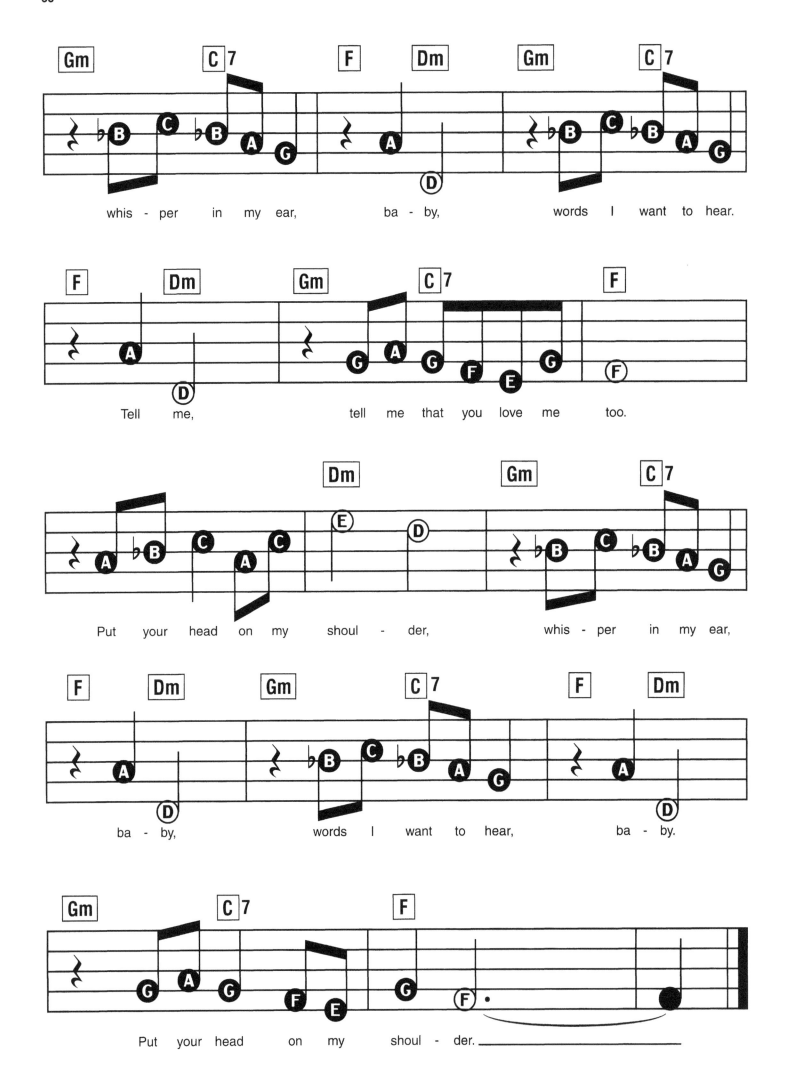

This page is intentionally left blank to eliminate a page turn.

Arrivederci, Roma
(Goodbye to Rome)
from the Motion Picture SEVEN HILLS OF ROME

Regi-Sound Program: 7
Rhythm: Rhumba

Words and Music by Carl Sigman, Ranucci Renato,
Sandro Giovanni and Peidro Garinei

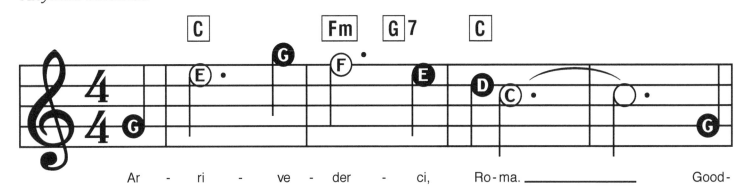

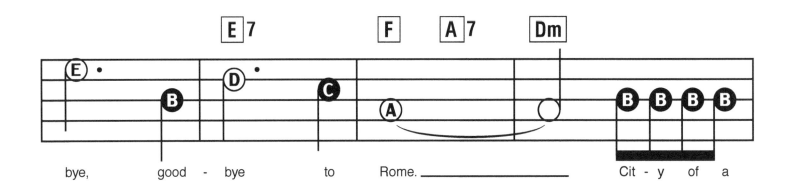

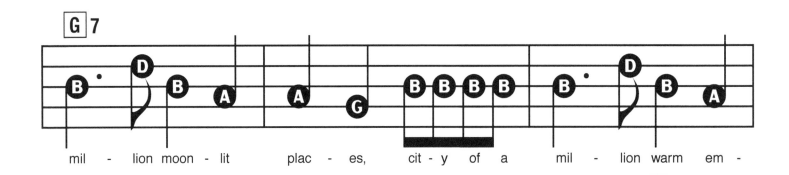

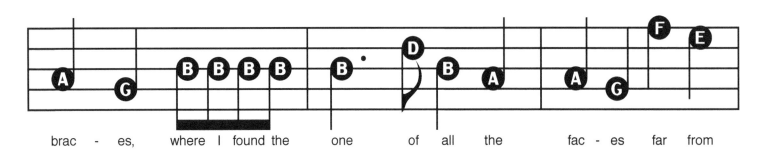

Copyright © 1954, 1955 (Renewed) by Music Sales Corporation (ASCAP) and EMI Music Publishing Italia SRL
All Rights for EMI Music Publishing Italia SRL in the U.S. and Canada Controlled and Administered by EMI April Music Inc. (ASCAP)
International Copyright Secured   All Rights Reserved
Reprinted by Permission

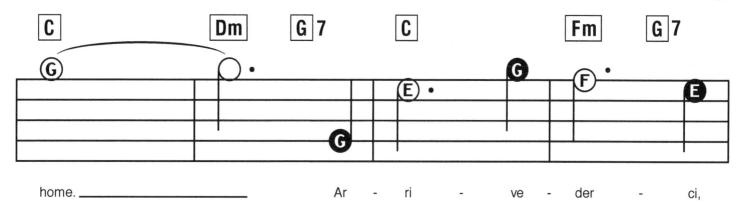

home. _____ Ar - ri - ve - der - ci,

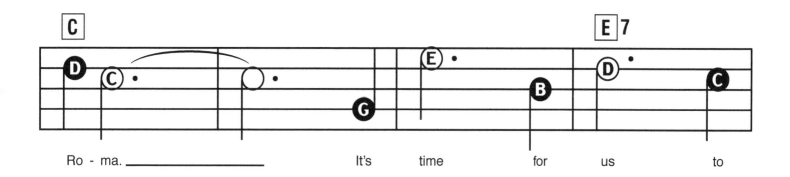

Ro - ma. _____ It's time for us to

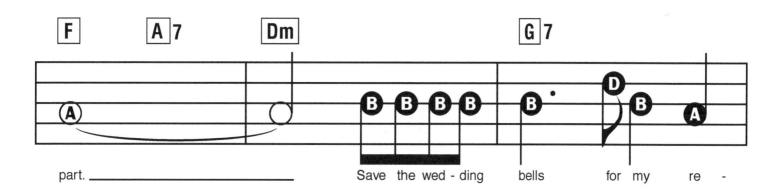

part. _____ Save the wed - ding bells for my re -

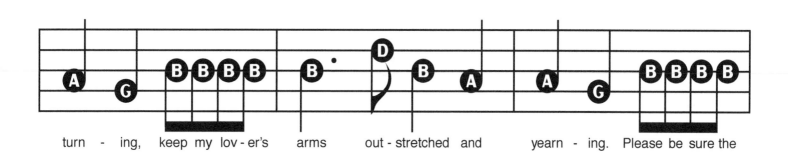

turn - ing, keep my lov - er's arms out - stretched and yearn - ing. Please be sure the

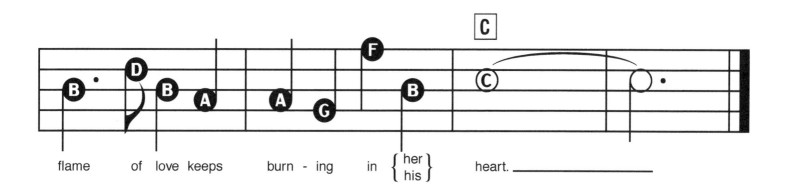

flame of love keeps burn - ing in { her / his } heart. _____

Bésame Mucho
(Kiss Me Much)

Regi-Sound Program: 1
Rhythm: Rhumba

Music and Spanish Words by Consuelo Velazquez
English Words by Sunny Skylar

Copyright © 1941, 1943 by Promotora Hispano Americana de Musica, S.A.
Copyrights Renewed
All Rights Administered by Peer International Corporation
International Copyright Secured   All Rights Reserved

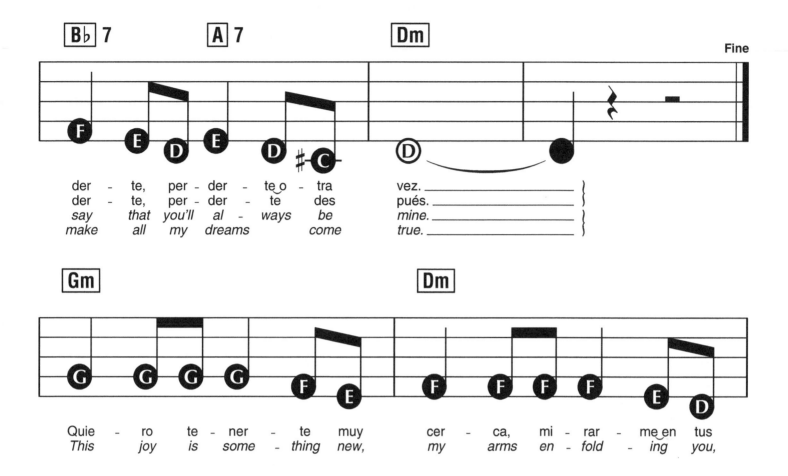

Fine

Bb 7	A 7	Dm

der - te, per - der - te o - tra vez. _____)
der - te, per - der - te des pués. _____)
say that you'll al - ways be mine. _____)
make all my dreams come true. _____)

Gm   Dm

Quie - ro te - ner - te muy cer - ca, mi - rar - me en tus
This joy is some - thing new, my arms en - fold - ing you,

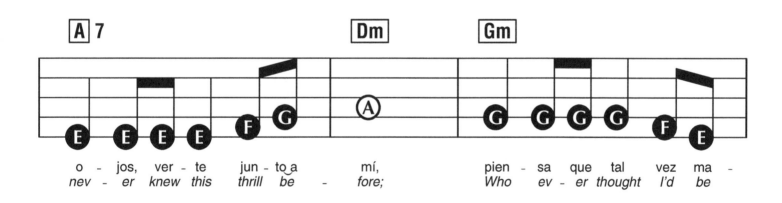

A 7   Dm   Gm

o - jos, ver - te jun - to a mí, pien - sa que tal vez ma -
nev - er knew this thrill be - fore; Who ev - er thought I'd be

D.C. al Fine
(Return to beginning
Play to Fine)

Dm   E 7   Bb 7   A 7

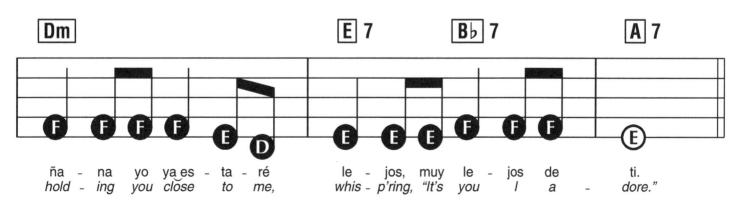

ña - na yo ya es - ta - ré le - jos, muy le - jos de ti.
hold - ing you close to me, whis - p'ring, "It's you I a - dore."

A Man Without Love
(Quando m'innamoro)

Regi-Sound Program: 8
Rhythm: Rhumba

English Lyric by Barry Mason
Original Words and Music by D. Pace,
M. Panzeri and R. Livraghi

I can re-mem-ber when we walked to-geth-er,_____

Shar-ing a love I thought would last for-ev-er._____

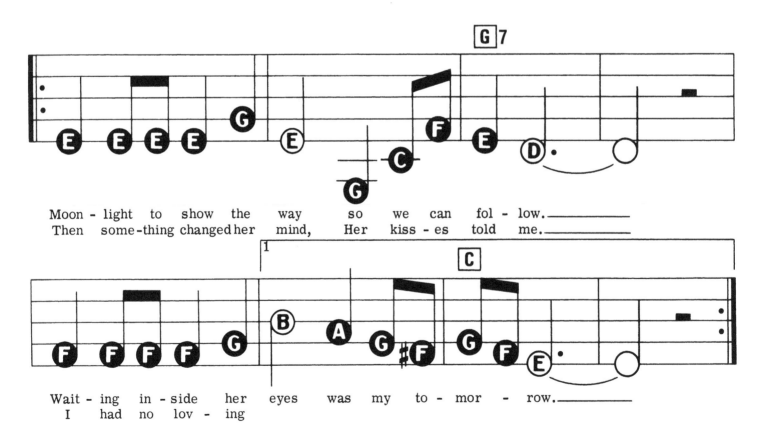

Moon-light to show the way so we can fol-low._____
Then some-thing changed her mind, Her kiss-es told me._____

Wait-ing in-side her eyes was my to-mor-row._____
I had no lov-ing

Copyright © 1968 EDIZIONI MUSICALI FIERA
Copyright Renewed
All Rights in the United States and Canada Controlled and Administered by UNIVERSAL MUSIC CORP.
All Rights Reserved   Used by Permission

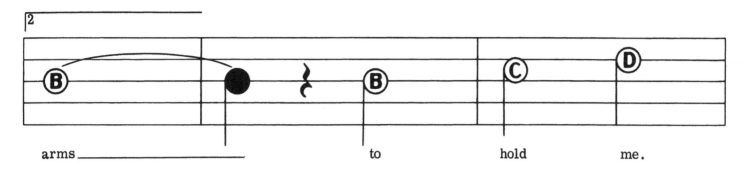

arms_____ to hold me.

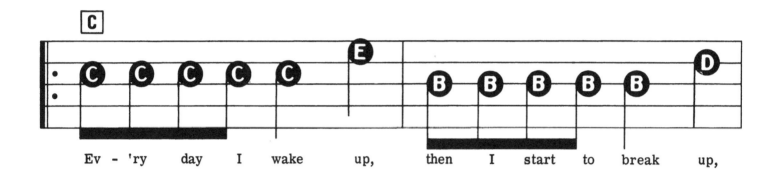

Ev - 'ry day I wake up, then I start to break up,

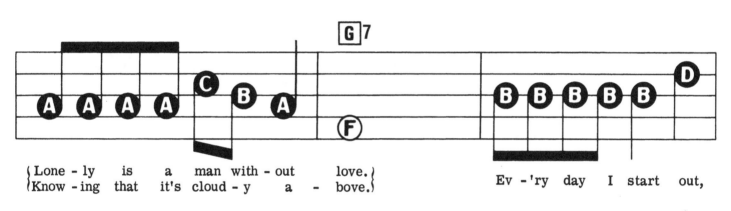

Lone - ly is a man with - out love.
Know - ing that it's cloud - y a - bove.
Ev - 'ry day I start out,

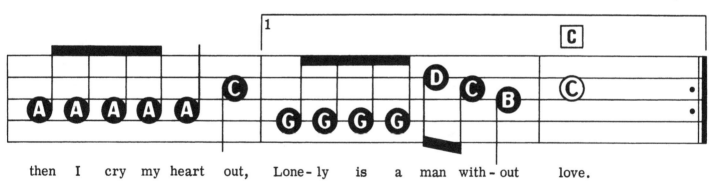

then I cry my heart out, Lone - ly is a man with - out love.

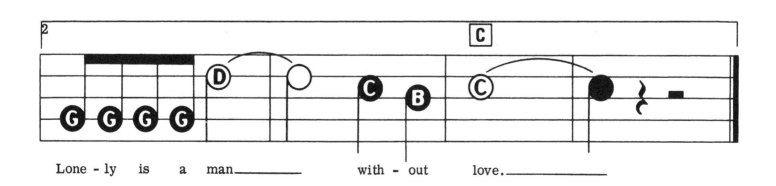

Lone - ly is a man_____ with - out love._____

Fly Me to the Moon
(In Other Words)

Regi-Sound Program: 8
Rhythm: Swing

Words and Music by
Bart Howard

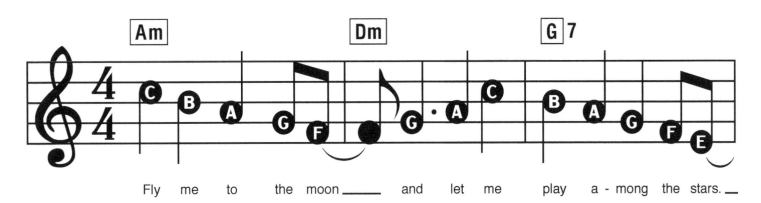

Fly me to the moon _____ and let me play a - mong the stars. _____

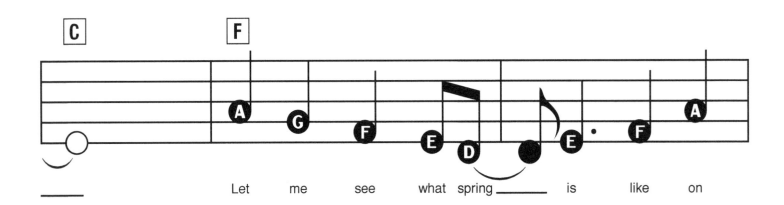

_____ Let me see what spring _____ is like on

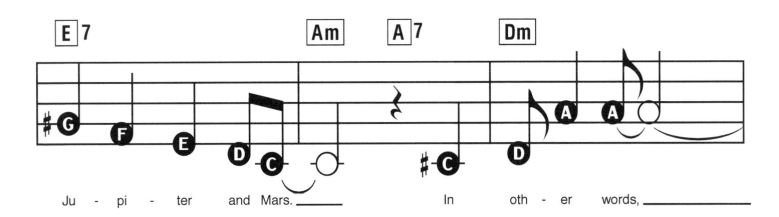

Ju - pi - ter and Mars. _____ In oth - er words, _____

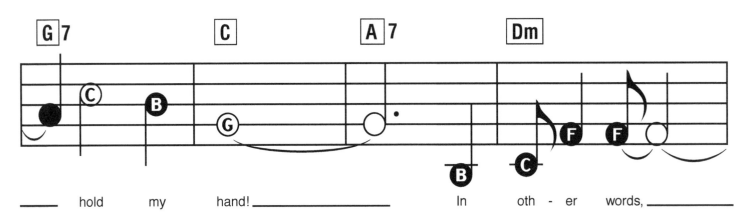

_____ hold my hand! _____ In oth - er words, _____

TRO - © Copyright 1954 (Renewed) Hampshire House Publishing Corp., New York, NY
International Copyright Secured
All Rights Reserved Including Public Performance For Profit
Used by Permission

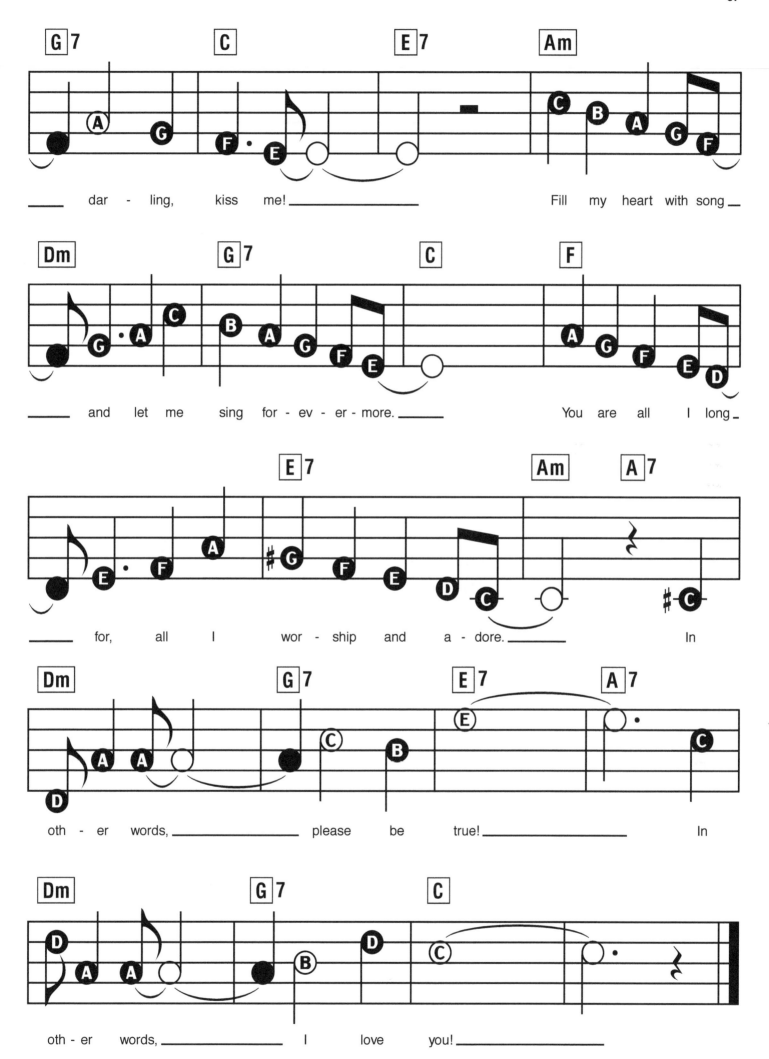

Look to the Rainbow
from FINIAN'S RAINBOW

Regi-Sound Program: 3
Rhythm: Waltz

Words by E.Y. "Yip" Harburg
Music by Burton Lane

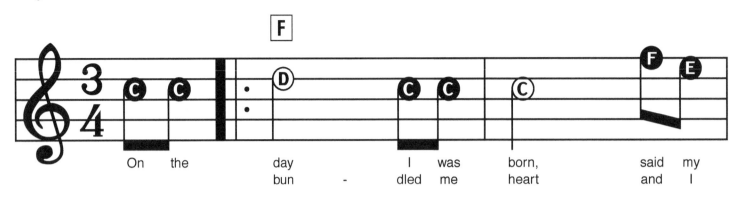

On the   day   I was born,   said my
bun - dled me heart   and I

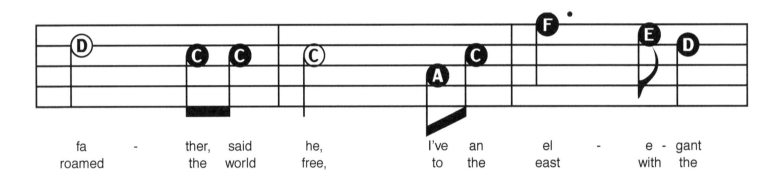

fa - ther,   said   he,   I've an   el - e - gant
roamed   the   world free,   to the   east   with the

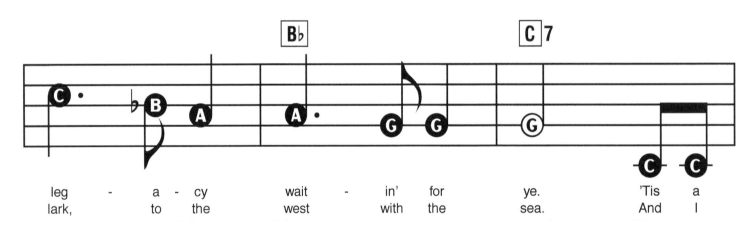

leg - a - cy   wait - in' for   ye.   'Tis a
lark,   to the   west   with the   sea.   And I

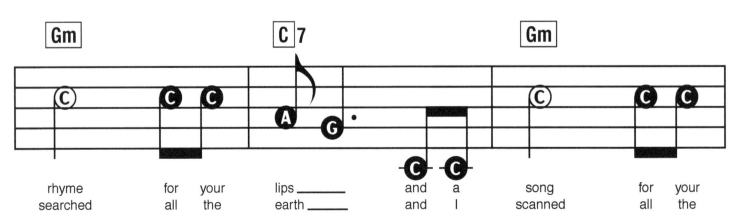

rhyme   for your   lips _____   and a   song   for your
searched   all the   earth _____   and I   scanned   all the

Copyright © 1946, 1947 by Chappell & Co. and Glocca Morra Music
Copyright Renewed
All Rights for Glocca Morra Music Administered by Next Decade Entertainment, Inc.
International Copyright Secured   All Rights Reserved

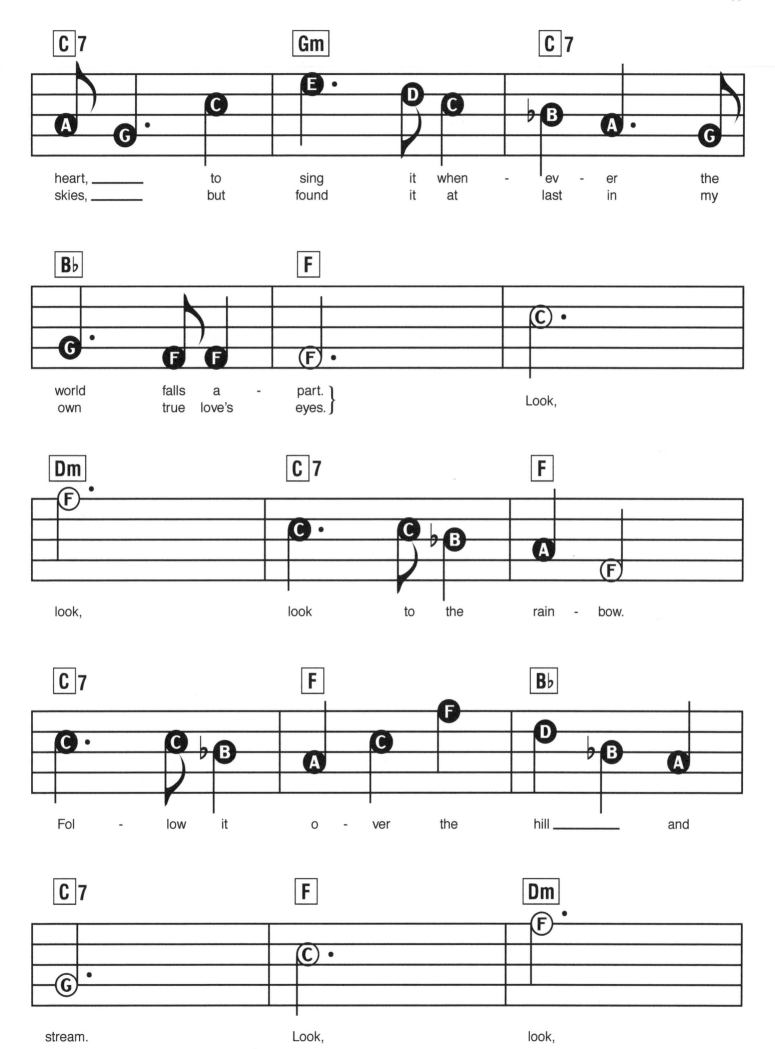

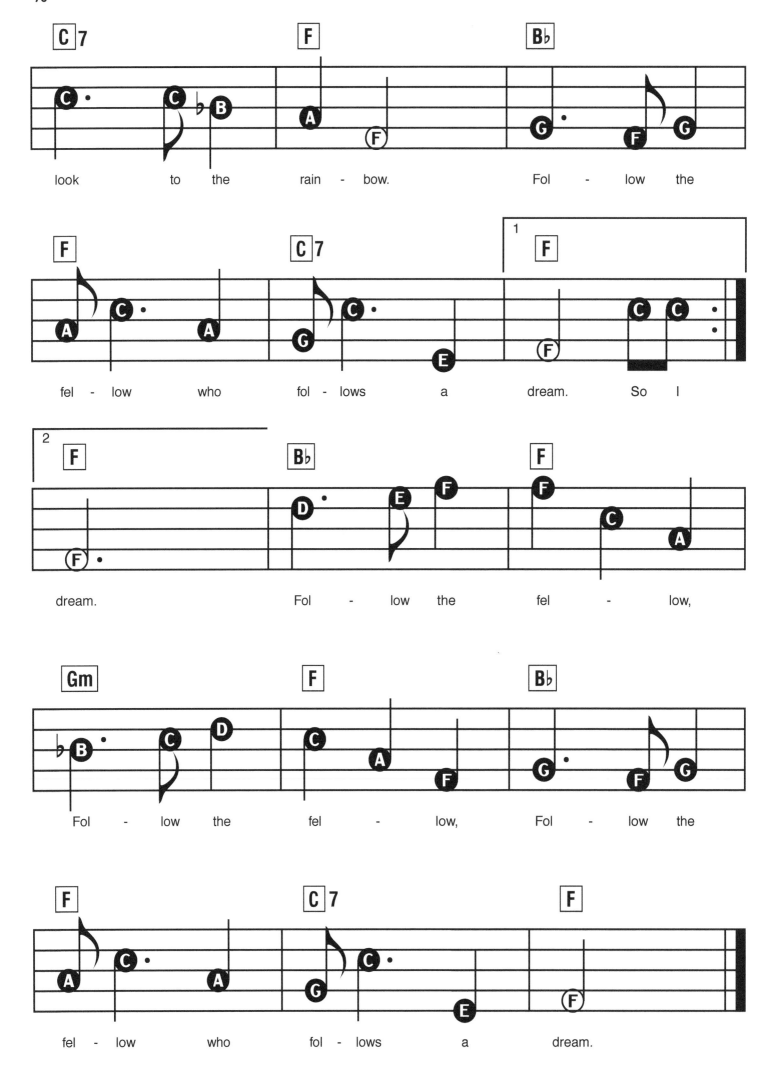

St. Thomas

Regi-Sound Program: 5
Rhythm: Calypso or Latin

By Sonny Rollins

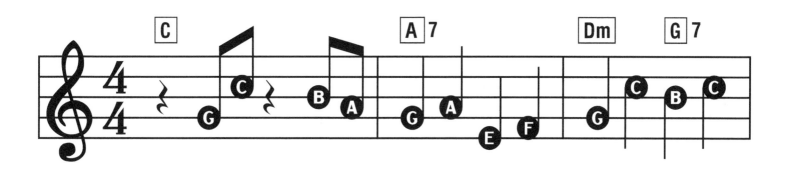

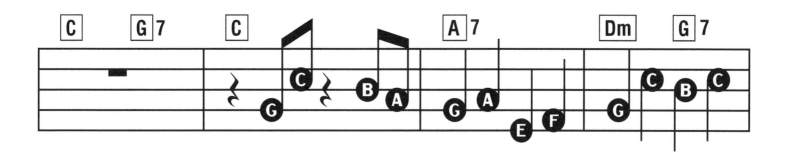

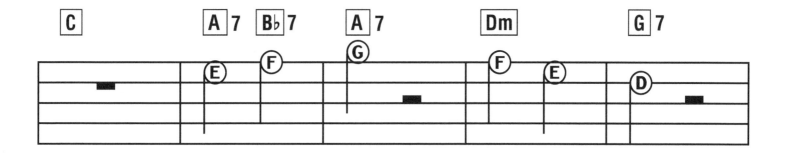

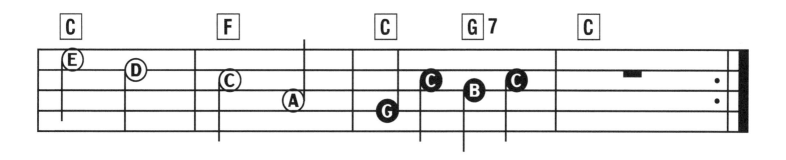

Copyright © 1963 Prestige Music
Copyright Renewed
International Copyright Secured   All Rights Reserved

Mambo Jambo
(Que rico el mambo)

Regi-Sound Program: 5
Rhythm: Mambo, Samba or Latin

English Words by Raymond Karl
and Charlie Towne
Original Words and Music by
Damaso Perez Prado

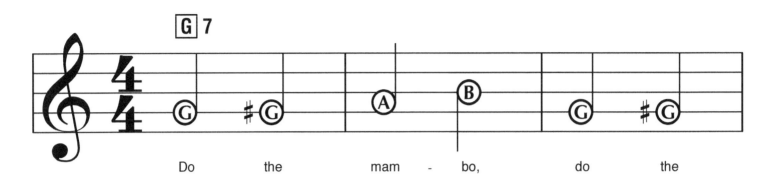

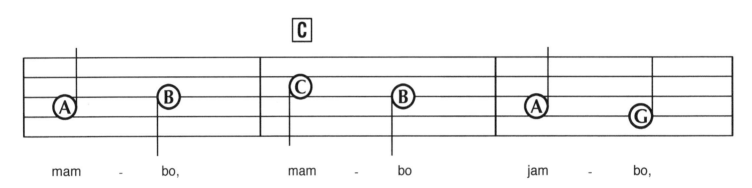

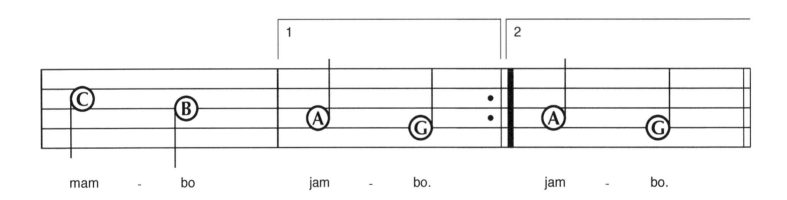

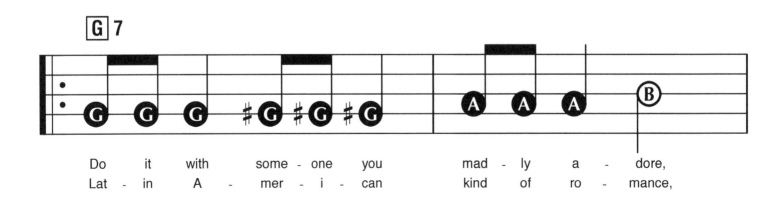

Copyright © 1950 by Peer International Corporation
Copyright Renewed
International Copyright Secured All Rights Reserved

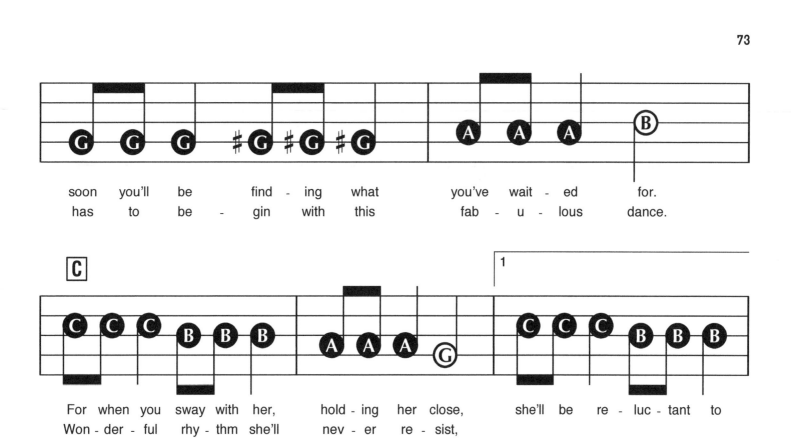

soon you'll be find - ing what you've wait - ed for.
has to be - gin with this fab - u - lous dance.

C

1

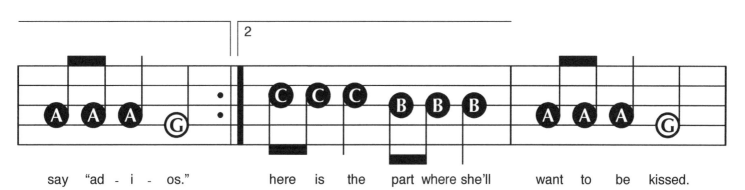

For when you sway with her, hold - ing her close, she'll be re - luc - tant to
Won - der - ful rhy - thm she'll nev - er re - sist,

2

say "ad - i - os." here is the part where she'll want to be kissed.

G 7   C

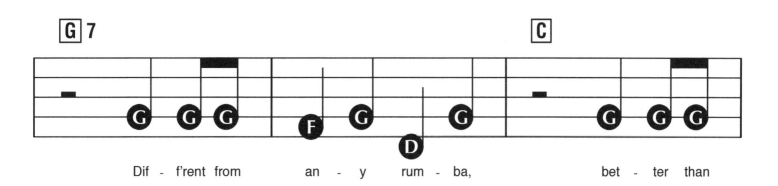

Dif - f'rent from an - y rum - ba, bet - ter than

G 7

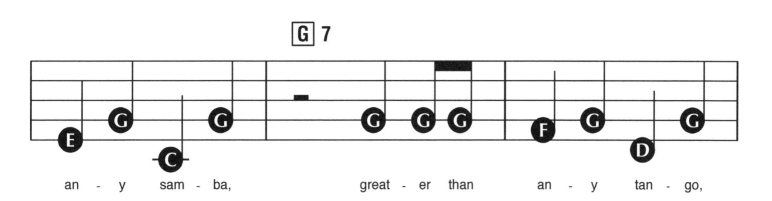

an - y sam - ba, great - er than an - y tan - go,

74

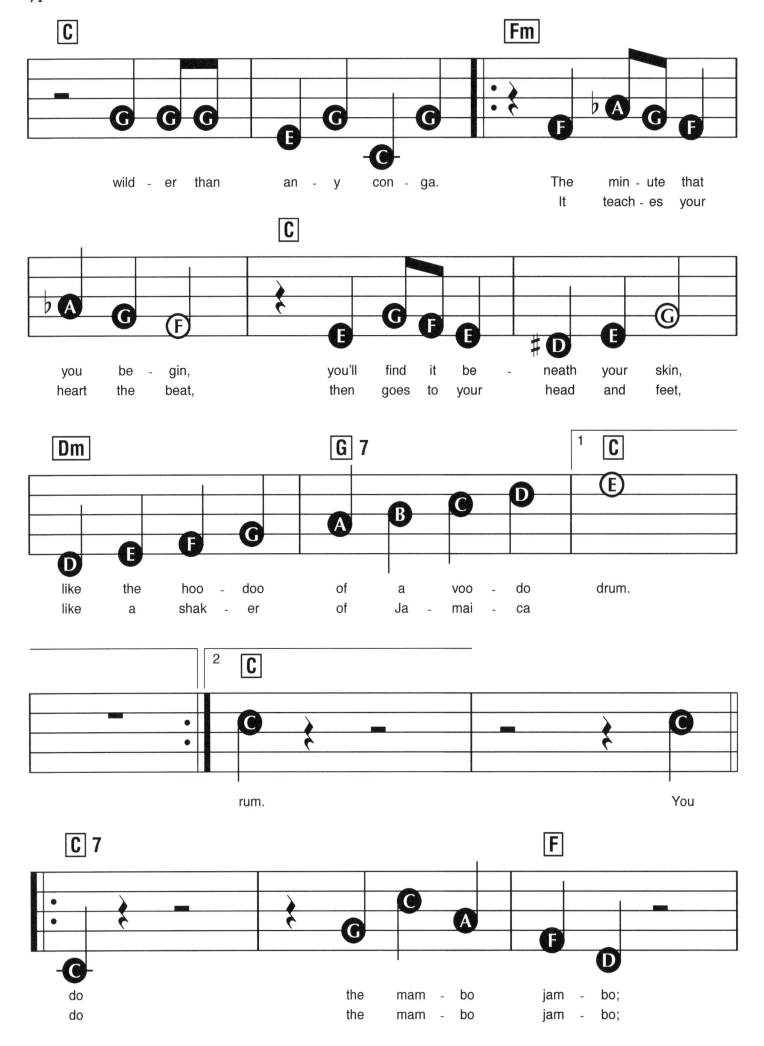

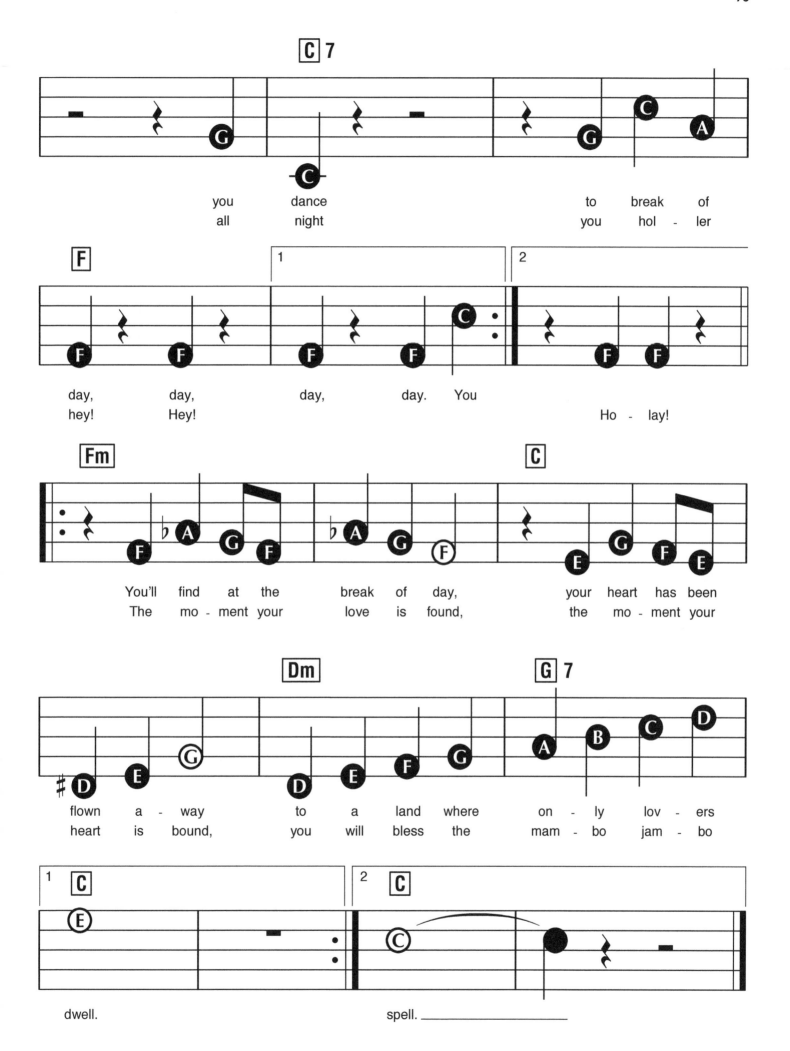

Born to Lose

Regi-Sound Program: 1
Rhythm: Country Swing or Fox Trot

Words and Music by
Ted Daffan

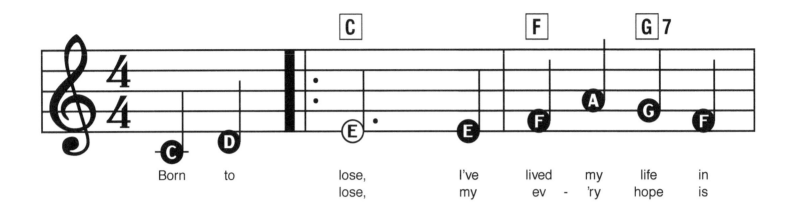

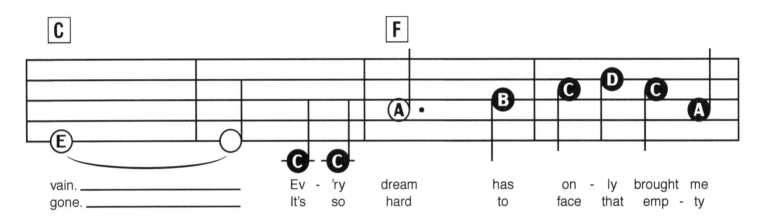

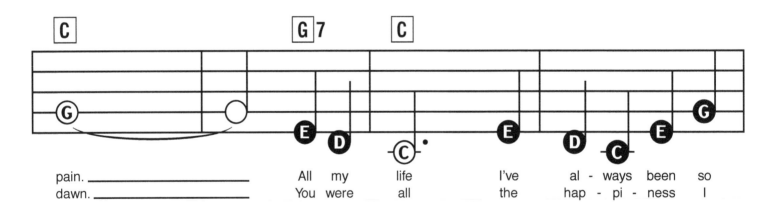

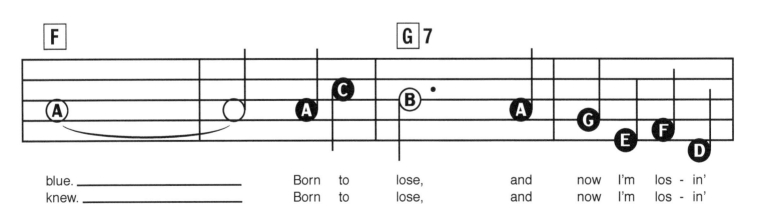

Copyright © 1943 by Peer International Corporation
Copyright Renewed
International Copyright Secured   All Rights Reserved

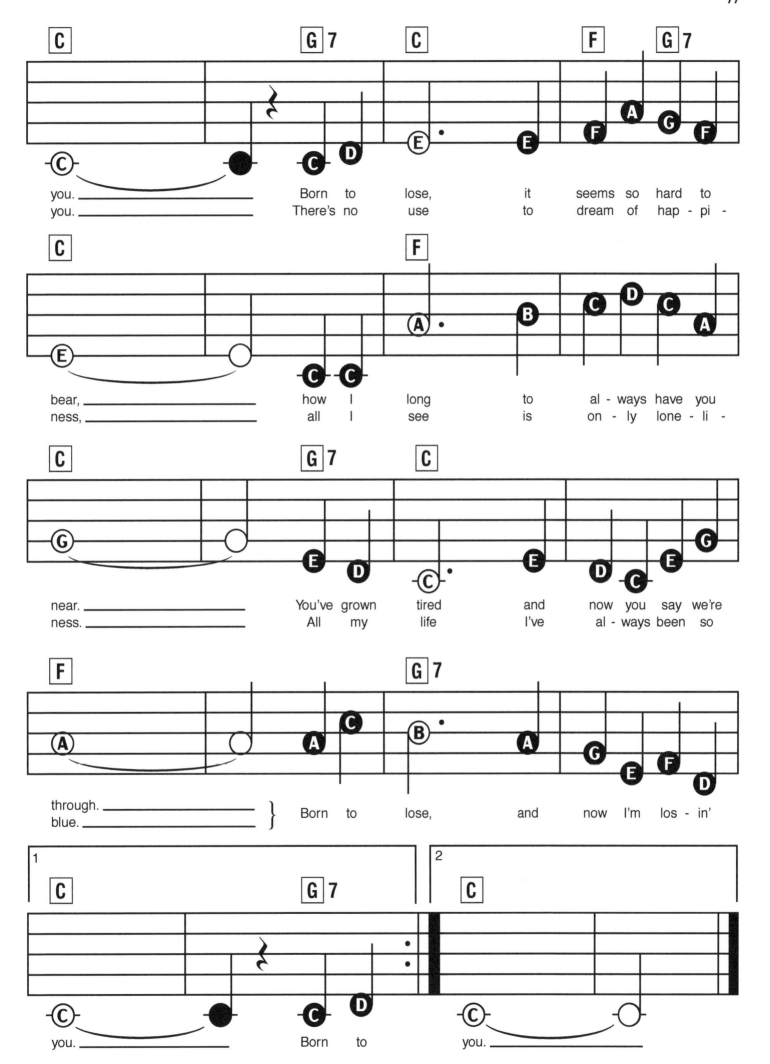

I Can't Stop Loving You

Regi-Sound Program: 8
Rhythm: Fox Trot or Country

Words and Music by
Don Gibson

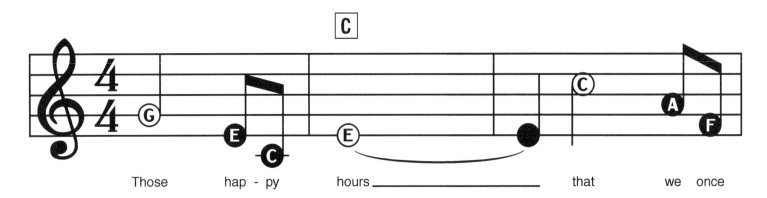

Those hap - py hours _____ that we once

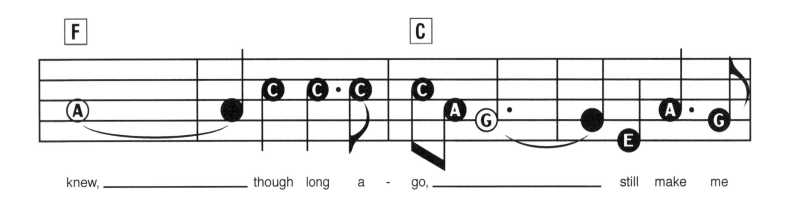

knew, _____ though long a - go, _____ still make me

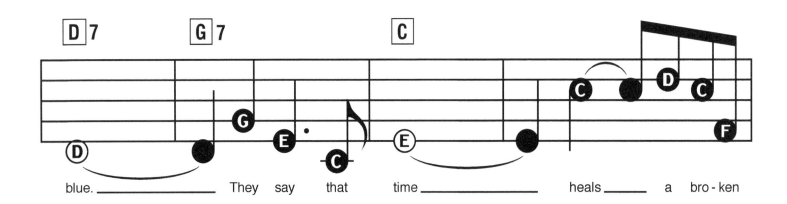

blue. _____ They say that time _____ heals _____ a bro - ken

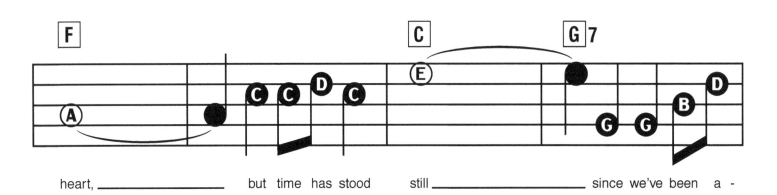

heart, _____ but time has stood still _____ since we've been a -

Copyright © 1958 Sony/ATV Music Publishing LLC
Copyright Renewed
All Rights Administered by Sony/ATV Music Publishing LLC,
 8 Music Square West, Nashville, TN 37203
International Copyright Secured All Rights Reserved

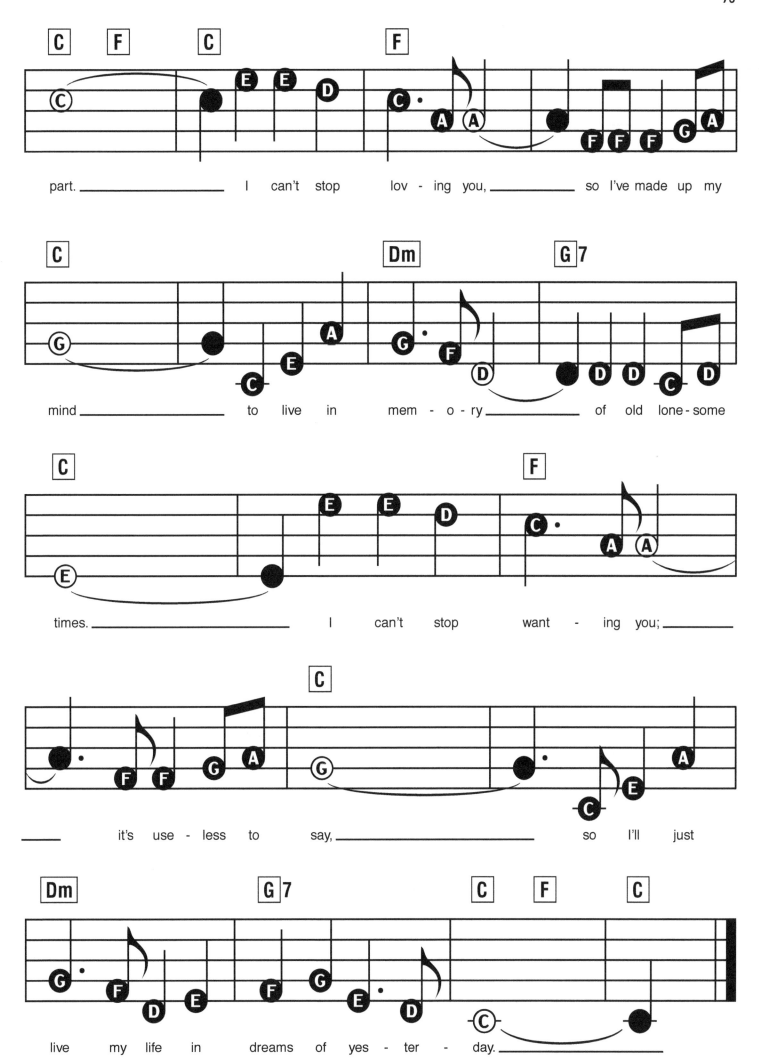

Stand by Me

Regi-Sound Program: 8
Rhythm: 8-Beat or Rock

Words and Music by Jerry Leiber,
Mike Stoller and Ben E. King

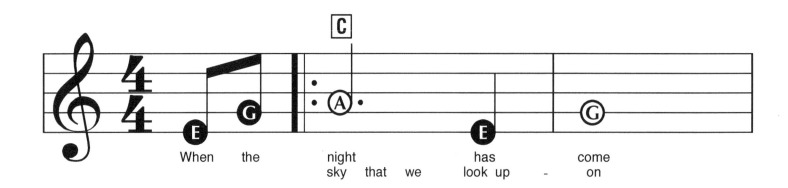

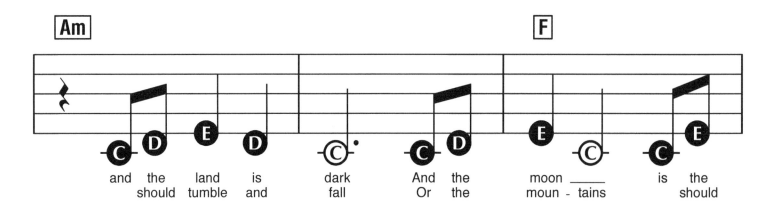

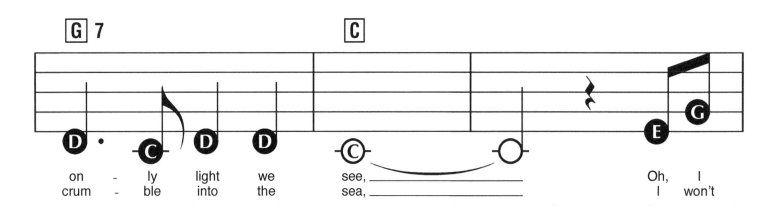

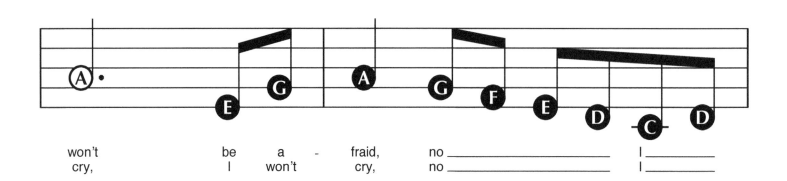

Copyright © 1961 Sony/ATV Music Publishing LLC
Copyright Renewed
All Rights Administered by Sony/ATV Music Publishing LLC, 8 Music Square West, Nashville, TN 37203
International Copyright Secured   All Rights Reserved

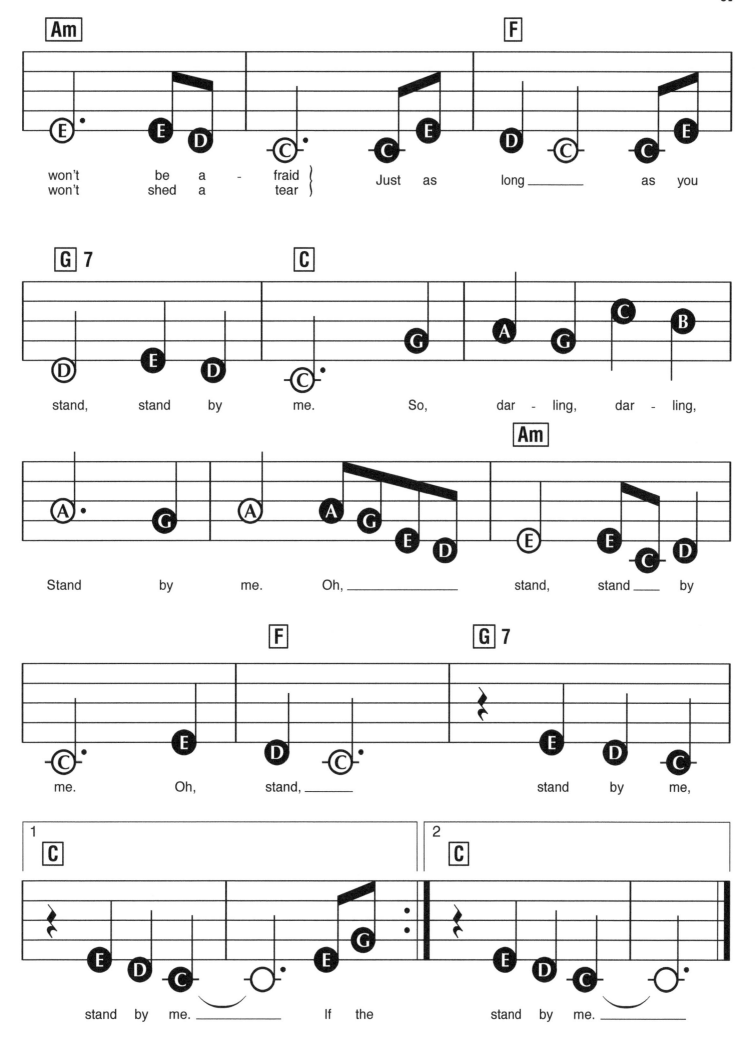

Unchained Melody
from the Motion Picture UNCHAINED

Regi-Sound Program: 3
Rhythm: None

Lyric by Hy Zaret
Music by Alex North

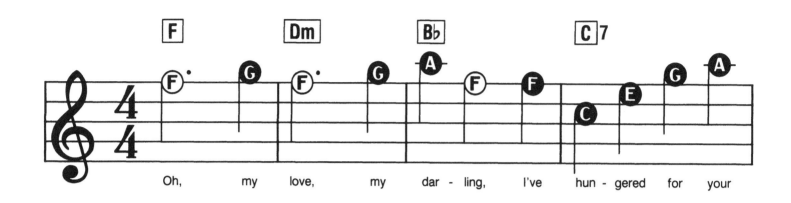

Oh, my love, my dar - ling, I've hun - gered for your

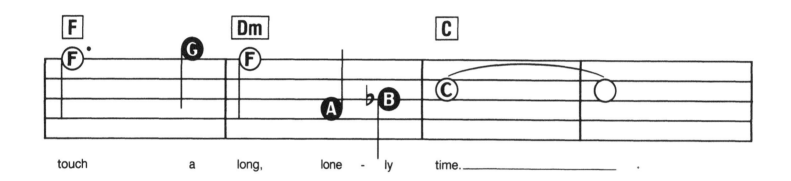

touch a long, lone - ly time. _____

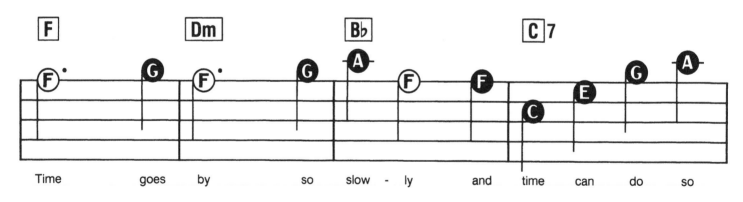

Time goes by so slow - ly and time can do so

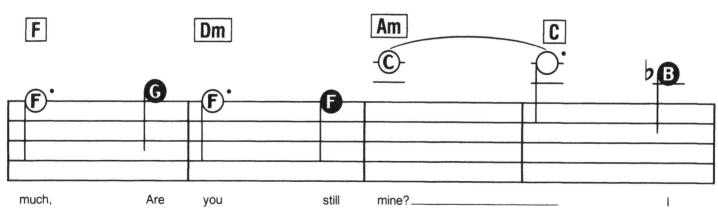

much, Are you still mine? _____   I

© 1955 (Renewed) FRANK MUSIC CORP.
All Rights Reserved

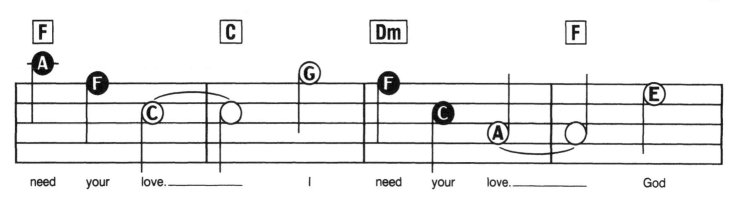

need your love. _____ I need your love. _____ God

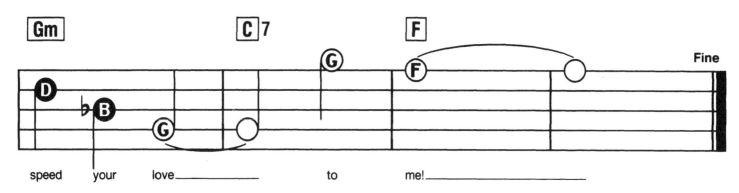

speed your love _____ to me! _____

Fine

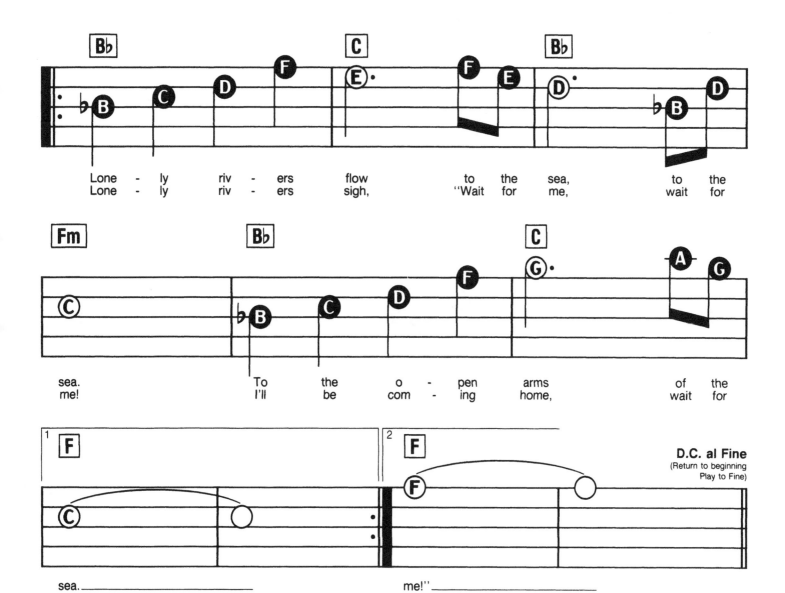

Lone - ly riv - ers flow to the sea, to the
Lone - ly riv - ers sigh, "Wait for me, wait for

sea. To the o - pen arms of the
me! I'll be com - ing home, wait for

D.C. al Fine
(Return to beginning
Play to Fine)

sea. _____ me!" _____

All Shook Up

Regi-Sound Program: 8
Rhythm: Rock 'n' Roll

Words and Music by Otis Blackwell
and Elvis Presley

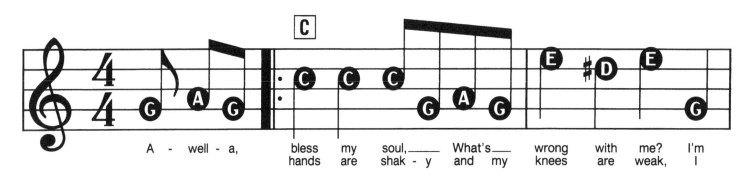

A - well - a, bless my soul,____ What's____ wrong with me? I'm

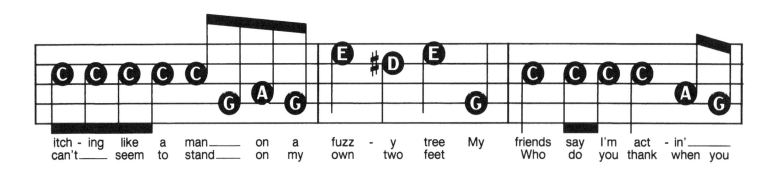

itch - ing like a man____ on a fuzz - y tree My friends say I'm act - in'____
can't____ seem to stand____ on my own two feet Who do you thank when you

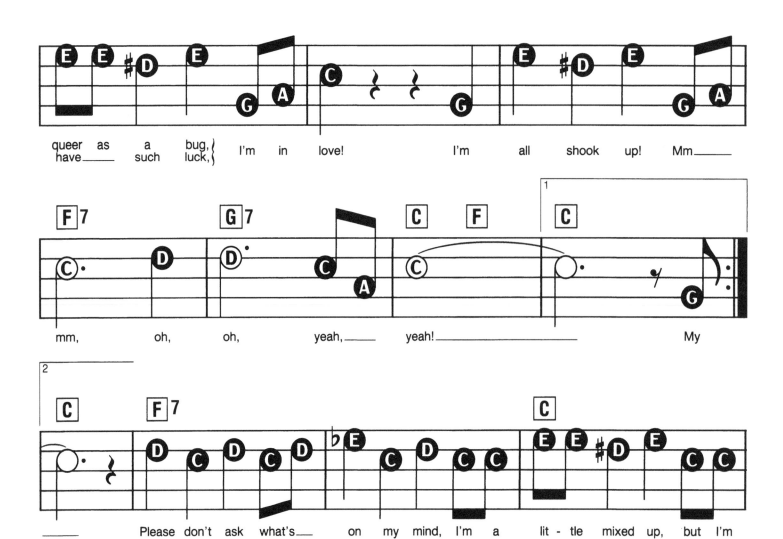

queer as a bug,} I'm in love! I'm all shook up! Mm____
have____ a such luck,}

mm, oh, oh, yeah,____ yeah! My

Please don't ask what's____ on my mind, I'm a lit - tle mixed up, but I'm

Copyright © 1957; Renewed 1985 Elvis Presley Music (BMI)
All Rights for Elvis Presley Music Administered by BMG Rights Management (US) LLC
International Copyright Secured   All Rights Reserved

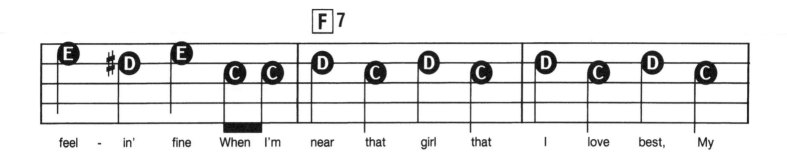

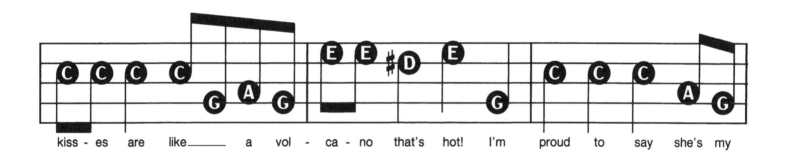

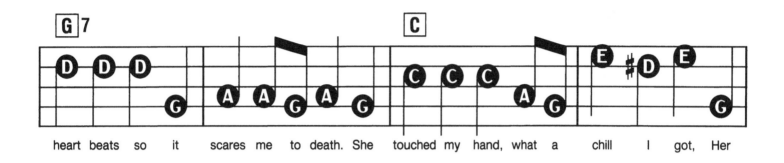

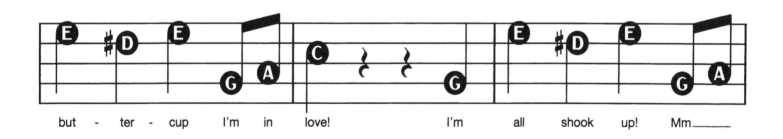

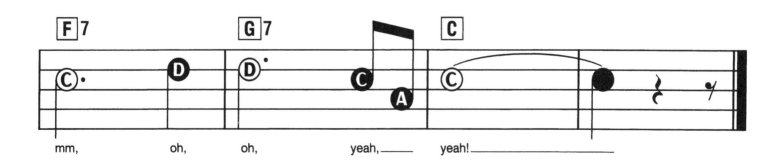

I Want to Hold Your Hand

Regi-Sound Program: 4
Rhythm: 8-Beat or Rock

Words and Music by John Lennon
and Paul McCartney

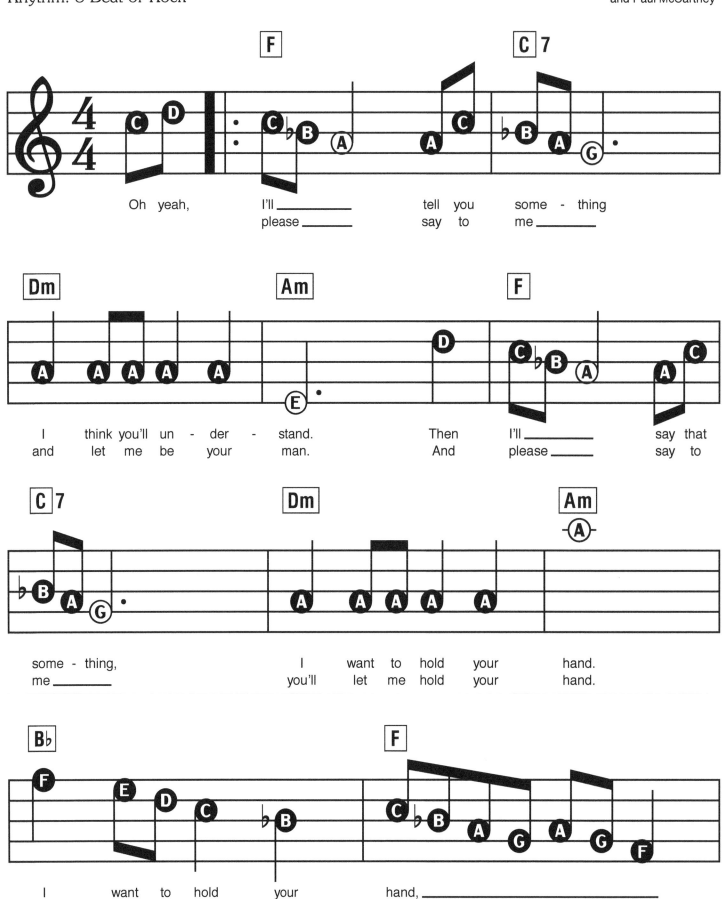

Copyright © 1963 NORTHERN SONGS LTD.
Copyright Renewed
All Rights in the United States and Canada Controlled and Administered by SONGS OF UNIVERSAL, INC.
All Rights Reserved   Used by Permission

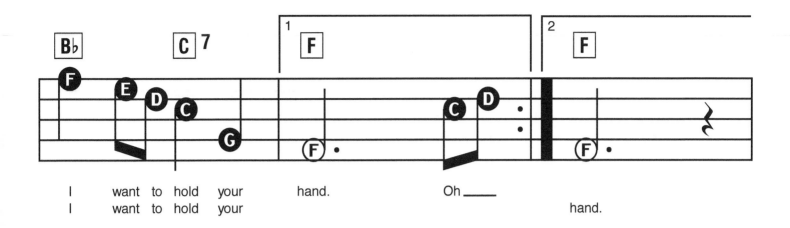

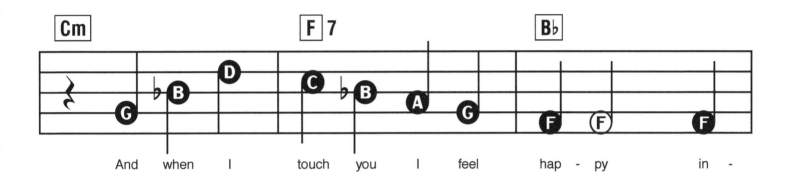

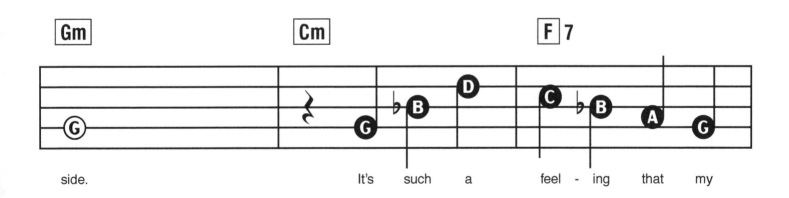

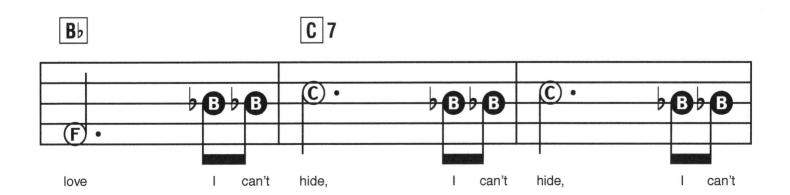

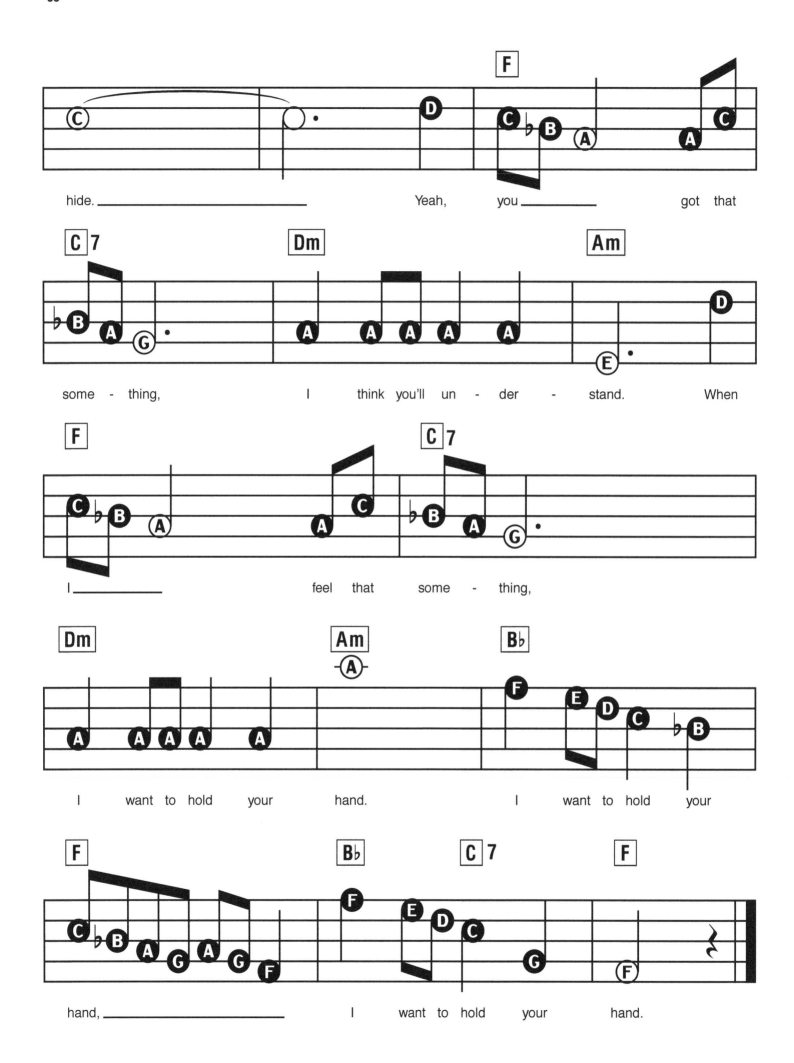

This page is intentionally left blank to eliminate a page turn.

We've Only Just Begun

Regi-Sound Program: 1
Rhythm: 8-Beat or Rock

Words and Music by Roger Nichols
and Paul Williams

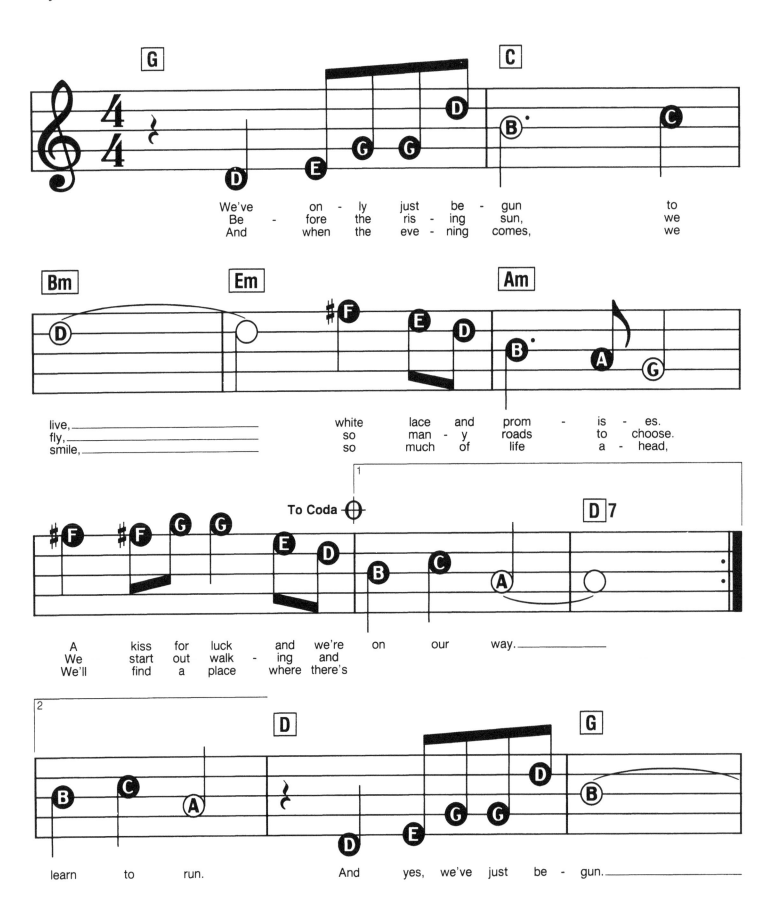

Copyright © 1970 IRVING MUSIC, INC.
Copyright Renewed
All Rights Reserved   Used by Permission

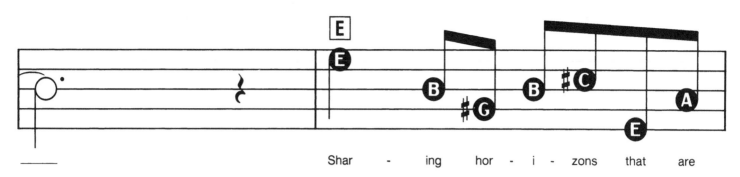

Shar - ing hor - i - zons that are

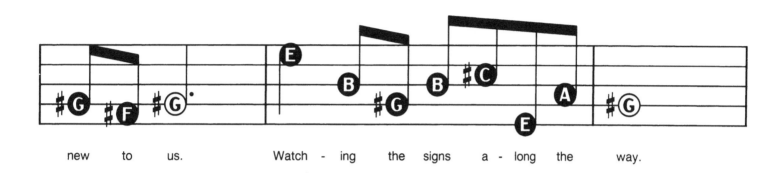

new to us. Watch - ing the signs a - long the way.

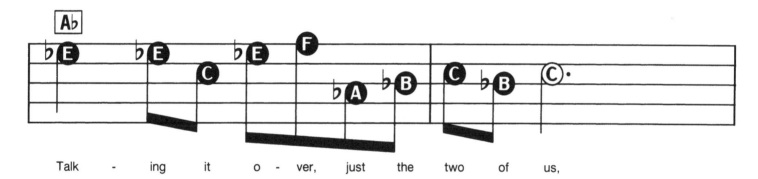

Talk - ing it o - ver, just the two of us,

D.C. al Coda
(Return to beginning
Play to ⊕ and
skip to Coda)

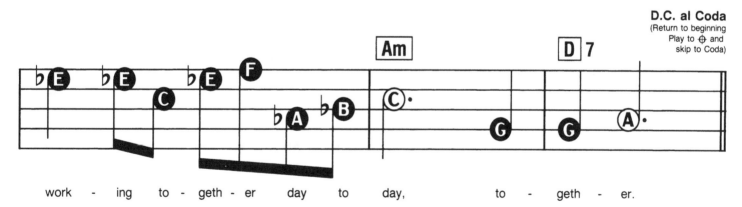

work - ing to - geth - er day to day, to - geth - er.

CODA

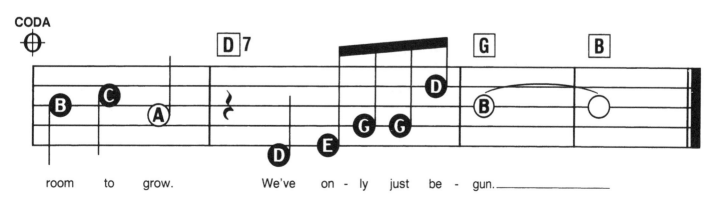

room to grow. We've on - ly just be - gun.

Sixteen Going On Seventeen
from THE SOUND OF MUSIC

Regi-Sound Program: 8
Rhythm: Fox Trot

Lyrics by Oscar Hammerstein II
Music by Richard Rodgers

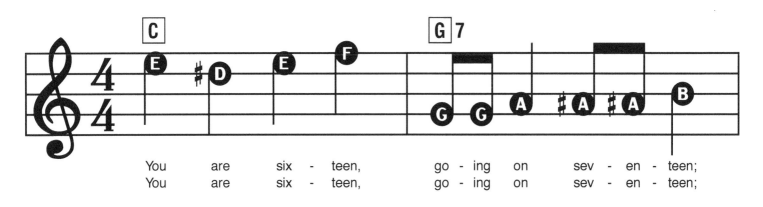

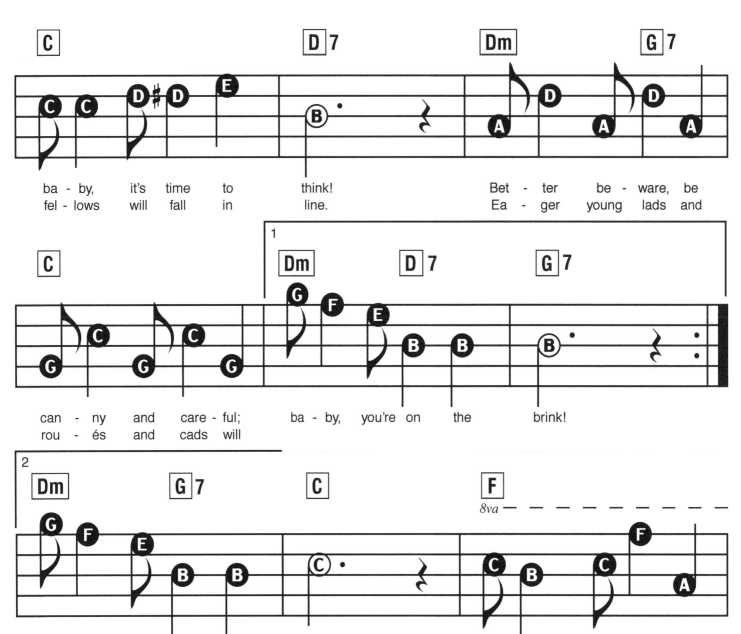

Copyright © 1959 by Richard Rodgers and Oscar Hammerstein II
Copyright Renewed
Williamson Music, a Division of Rodgers & Hammerstein: an Imagem Company, owner of publication and allied rights throughout the world
International Copyright Secured   All Rights Reserved

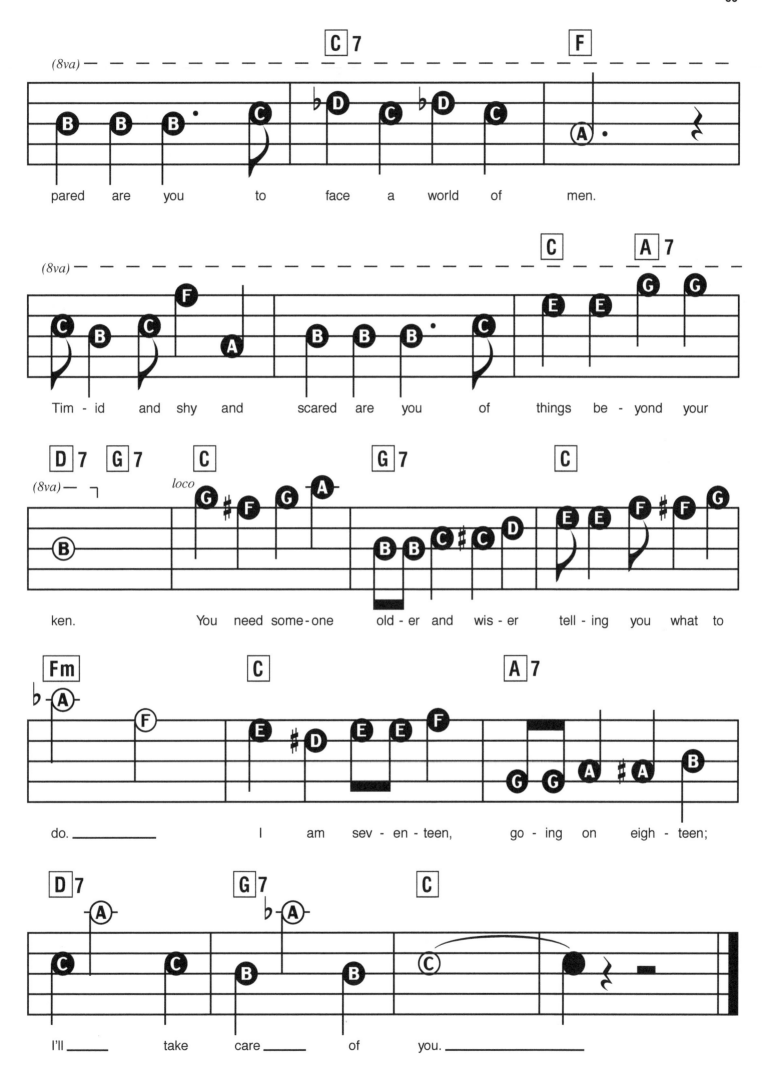

The Night Has a Thousand Eyes

Theme from the Paramount Picture
THE NIGHT HAS A THOUSAND EYES

Regi-Sound Program: 4
Rhythm: Bossa Nova

Words by Buddy Bernier
Music by Jerry Brainin

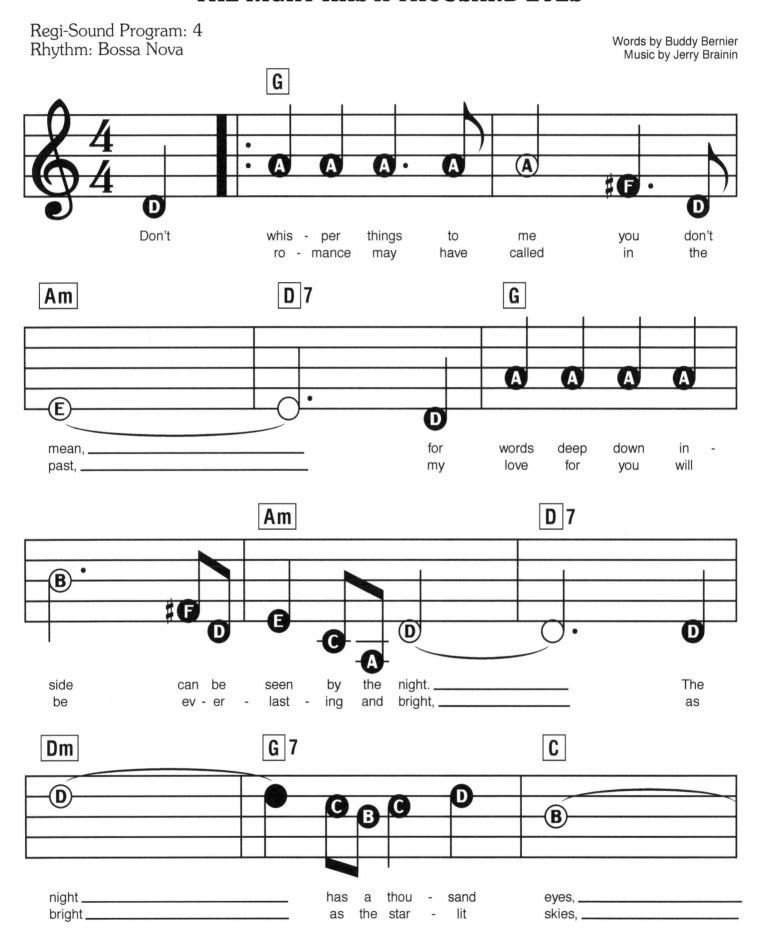

Copyright © 1948 Sony/ATV Music Publishing LLC
Copyright Renewed
All Rights Administered by Sony/ATV Music Publishing LLC, 8 Music Square West, Nashville, TN 37203
International Copyright Secured   All Rights Reserved

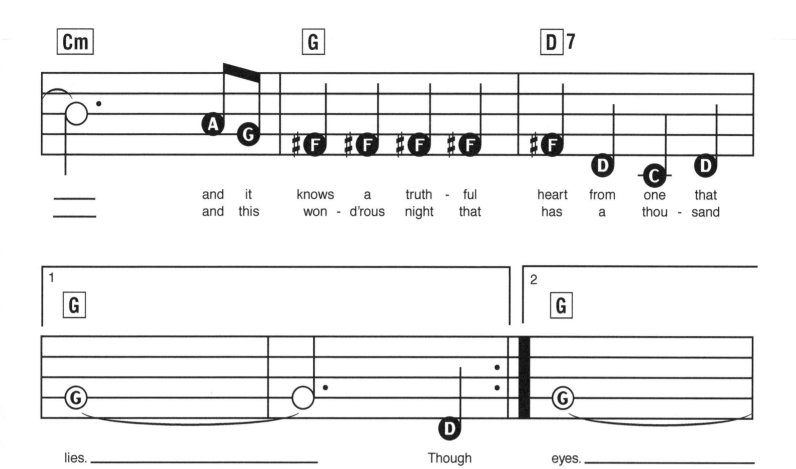

and it knows a truth - ful heart from one that
and this won - d'rous night that has a thou - sand

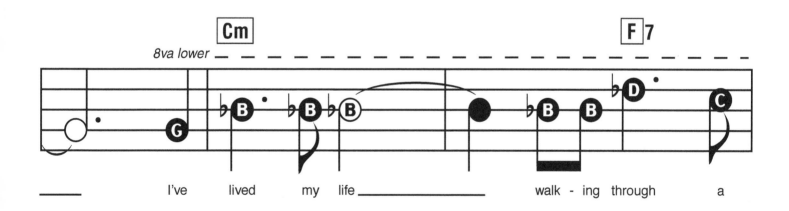

lies. _____ Though eyes. _____

I've lived my life _____ walk - ing through a

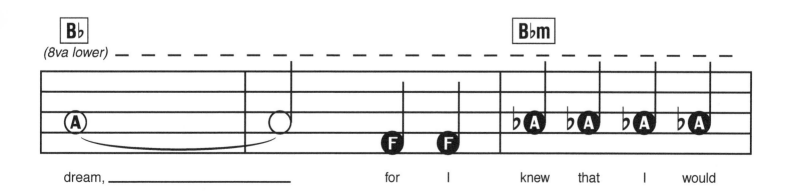

dream, _____ for I knew that I would

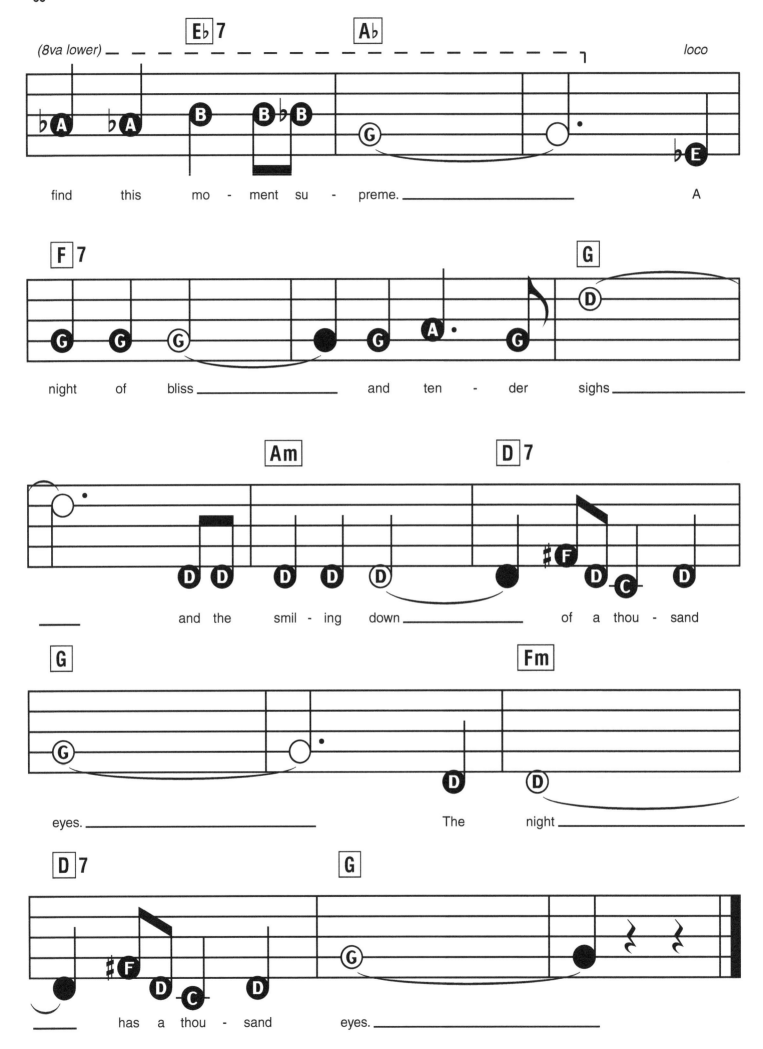

This page is intentionally left blank to eliminate a page turn.

Sing
from SESAME STREET

Regi-Sound Program: 8
Rhythm: Fox Trot

Words and Music by
Joe Raposo

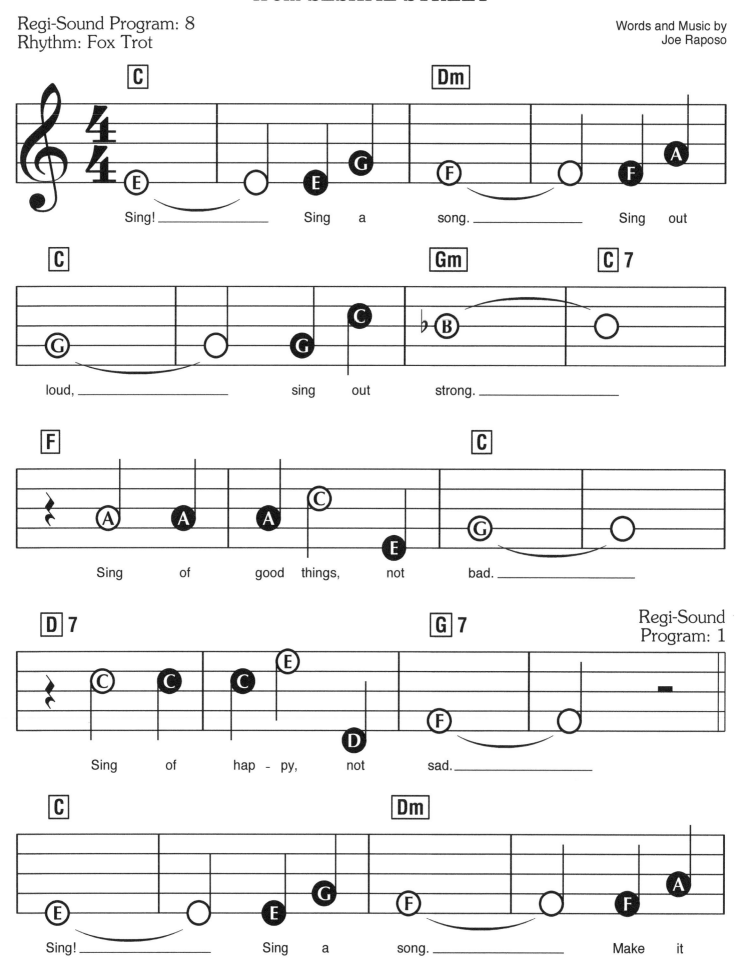

Copyright © 1971 by Jonico Music, Inc.
Copyright Renewed
All Rights in the U.S.A. Administered by Green Fox Music, Inc.
International Copyright Secured All Rights Reserved

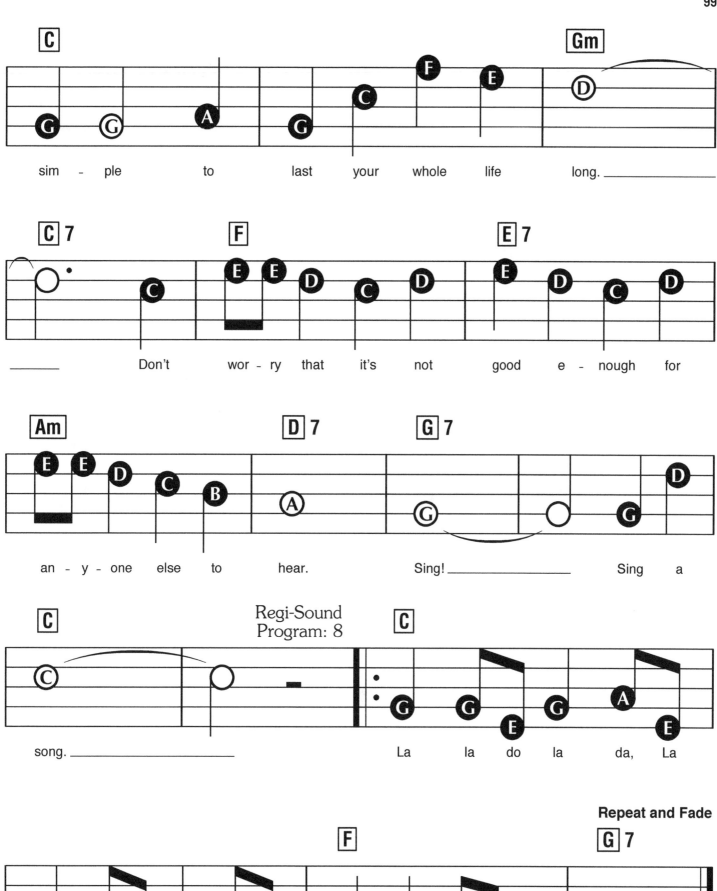

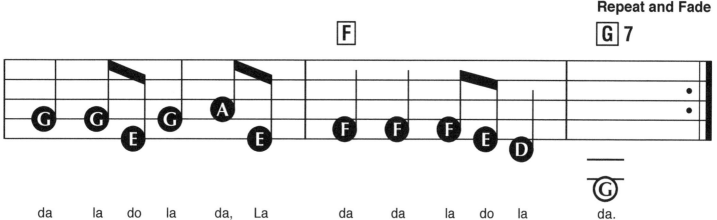

A Time for Us
(Love Theme)
from the Paramount Picture ROMEO AND JULIET

Regi-Sound Program: 1
Rhythm: Waltz

Words by Larry Kusik and Eddie Snyder
Music by Nino Rota

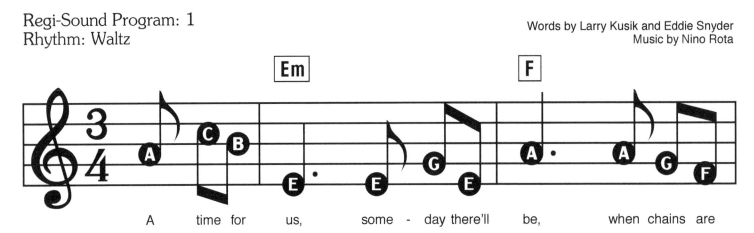

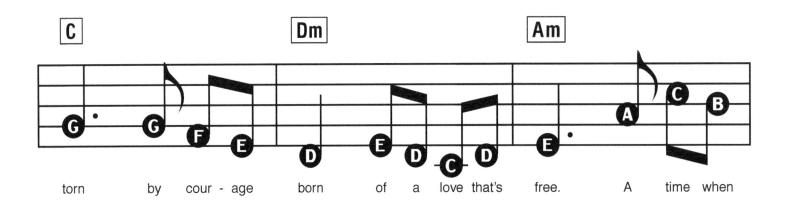

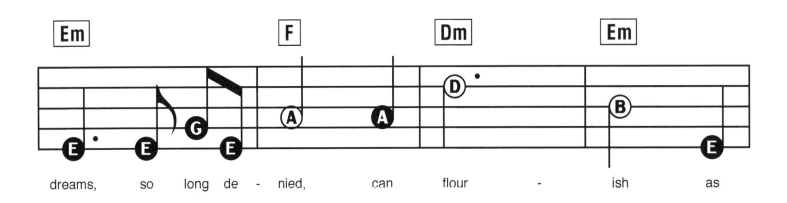

Regi-Sound
Program: 3

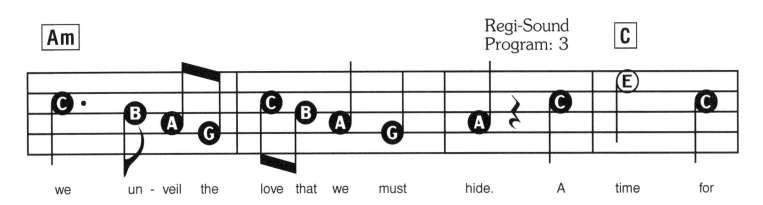

Copyright © 1968 Sony/ATV Music Publishing LLC
Copyright Renewed
All Rights Administered by Sony/ATV Music Publishing LLC,
  8 Music Square West, Nashville, TN 37203
International Copyright Secured   All Rights Reserved

101

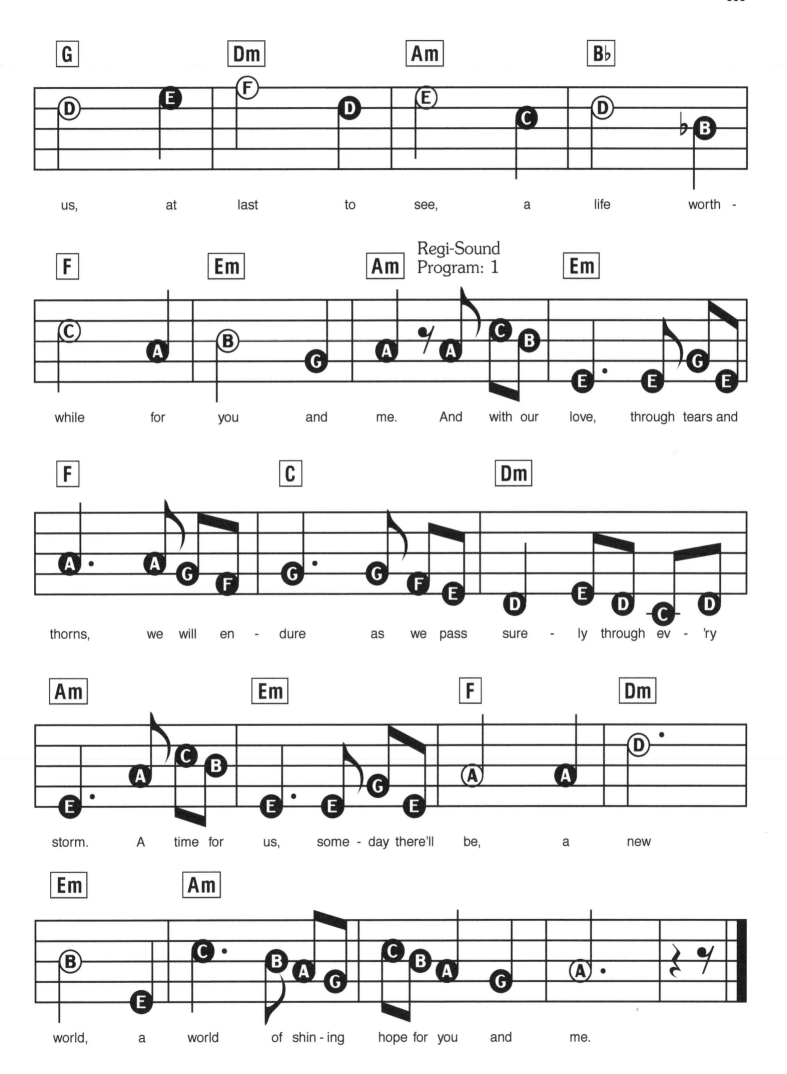

My Heart Will Go On
(Love Theme from 'Titanic')
from the Paramount and Twentieth Century Fox Motion Picture TITANIC

Regi-Sound Program: 8
Rhythm: Ballad

Music by James Horner
Lyric by Will Jennings

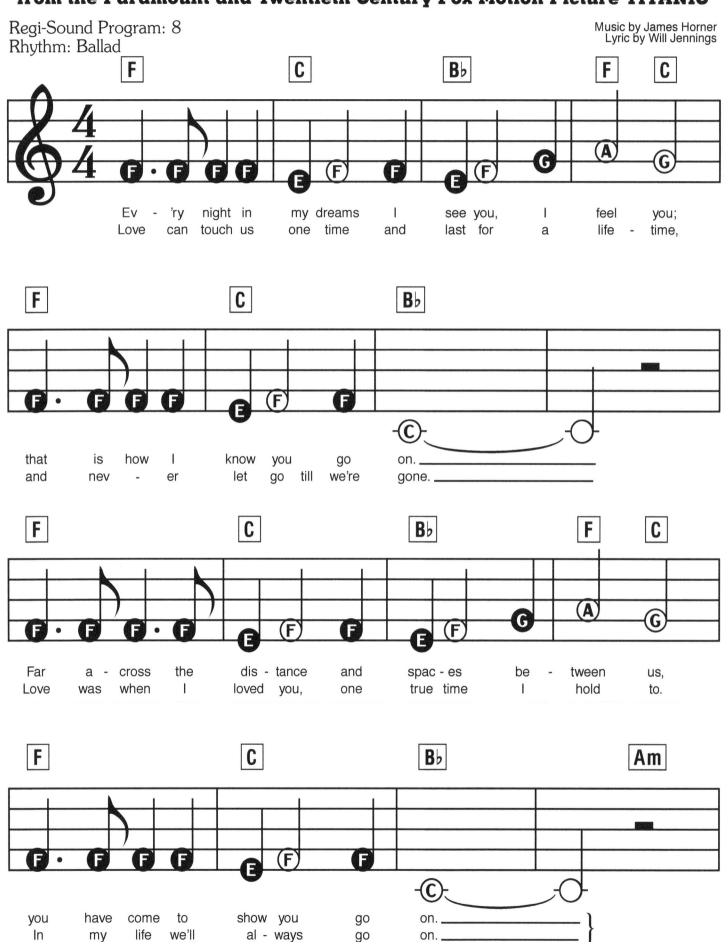

Copyright © 1997 Sony/ATV Music Publishing LLC, T C F Music Publishing, Inc., Fox Film Music Corporation and Blue Sky Rider Songs
All Rights on behalf of Sony/ATV Music Publishing LLC Administered by Sony/ATV Music Publishing LLC, 8 Music Square West, Nashville, TN 37203
All Rights on behalf of Blue Sky Rider Songs Administered by Irving Music, Inc.
International Copyright Secured   All Rights Reserved

Regi-Sound Program: 4

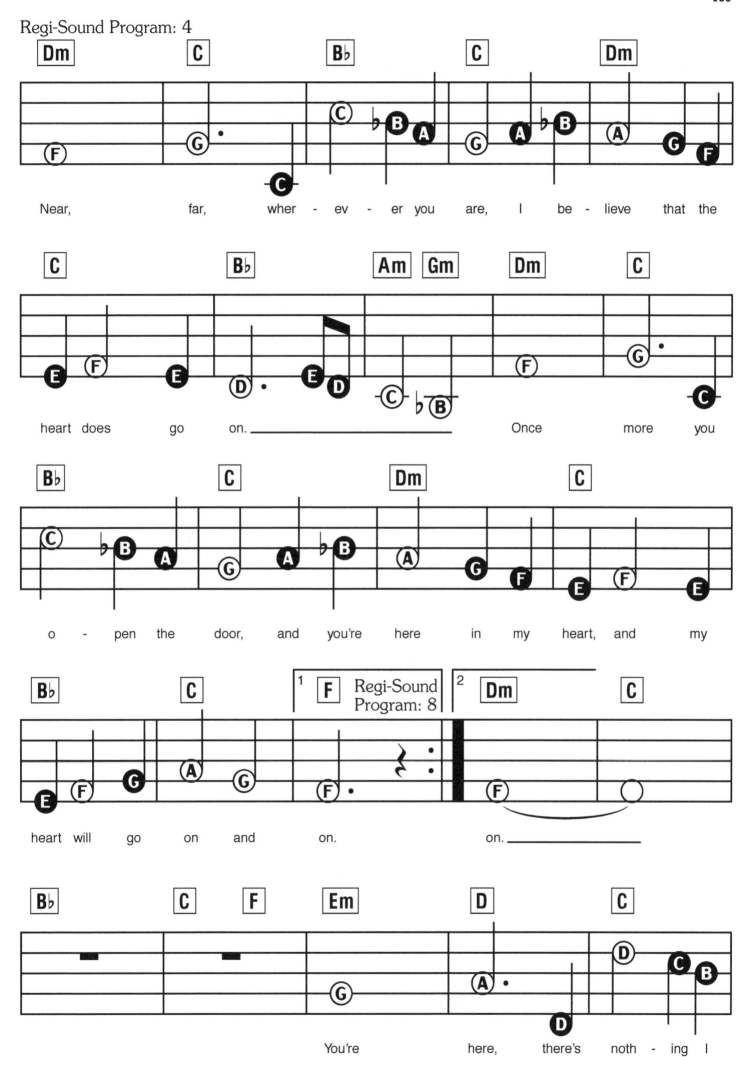

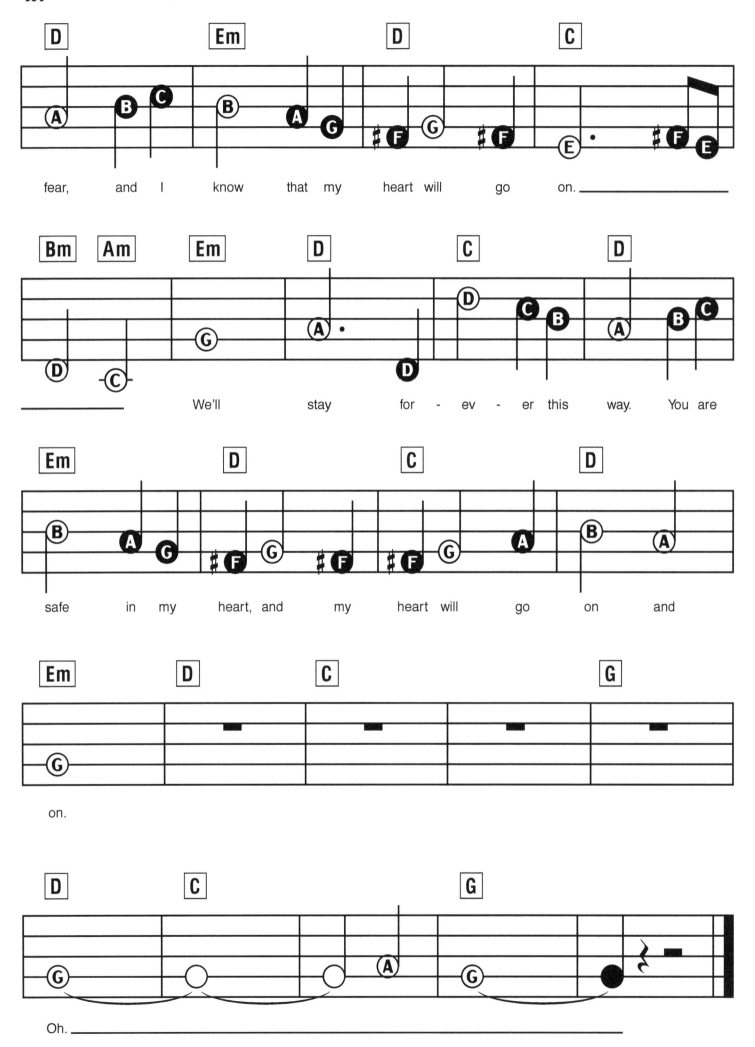

Raindrops Keep Fallin' on My Head

from BUTCH CASSIDY AND THE SUNDANCE KID

Regi-Sound Program: 1
Rhythm: Swing or Fox Trot

Lyric by Hal David
Music by Burt Bacharach

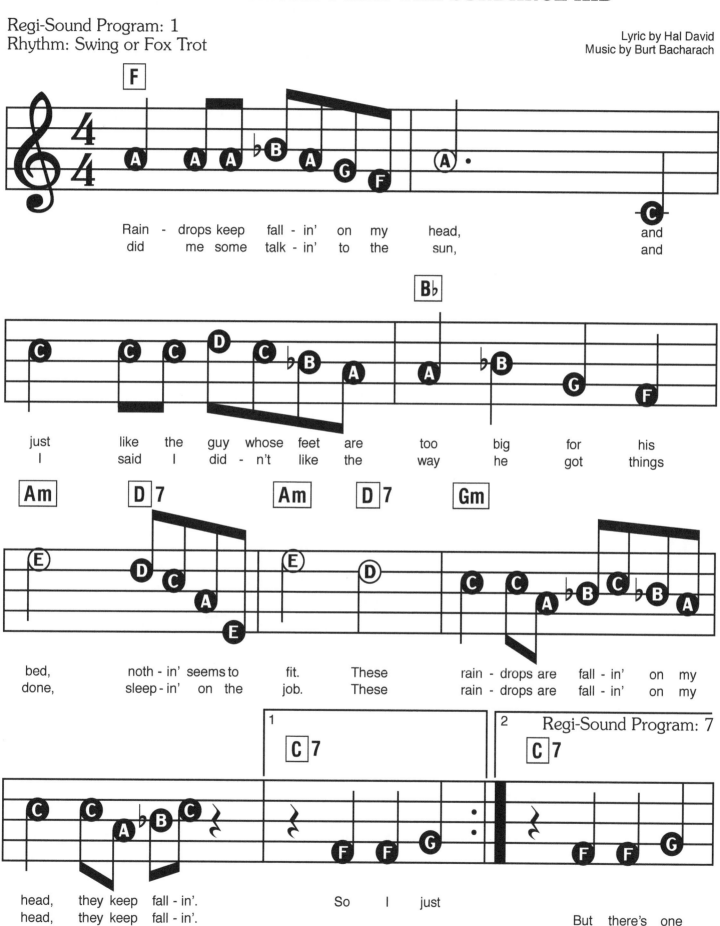

Copyright © 1969 (Renewed) Casa David, New Hidden Valley Music and WB Music Corp.
International Copyright Secured All Rights Reserved

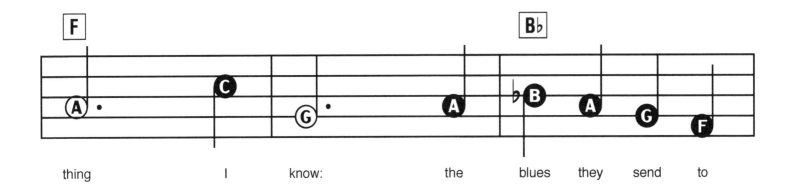

thing   I   know: the   blues   they   send   to

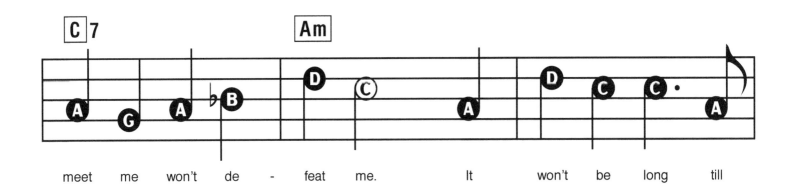

meet   me   won't   de -   feat   me.   It   won't   be   long   till

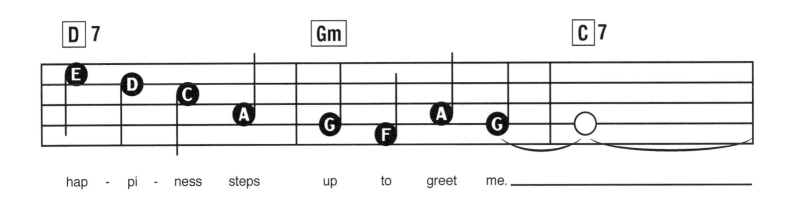

hap - pi - ness   steps   up   to   greet   me.

Regi-Sound
Program: 1

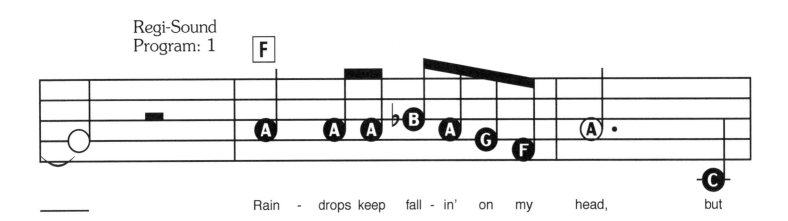

Rain - drops   keep   fall - in'   on   my   head,   but

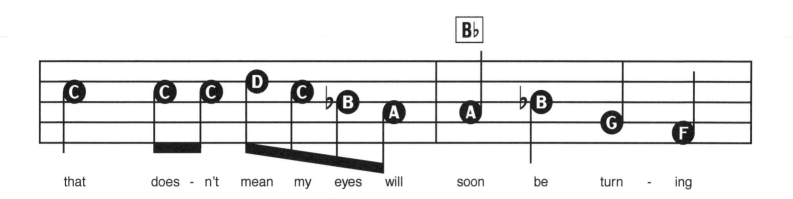

that   does - n't   mean   my   eyes   will   soon   be   turn - ing

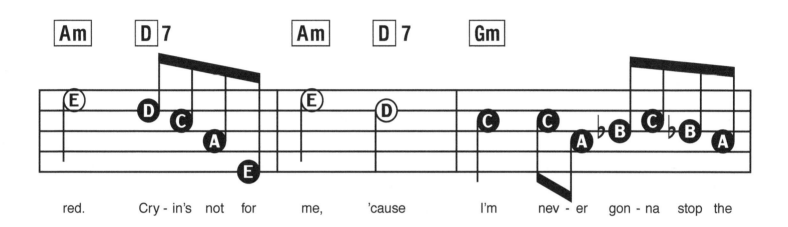

red.   Cry - in's   not   for   me,   'cause   I'm   nev - er   gon - na   stop   the

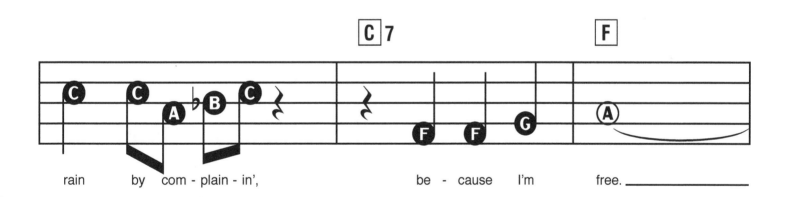

rain   by   com - plain - in',   be - cause   I'm   free. _____

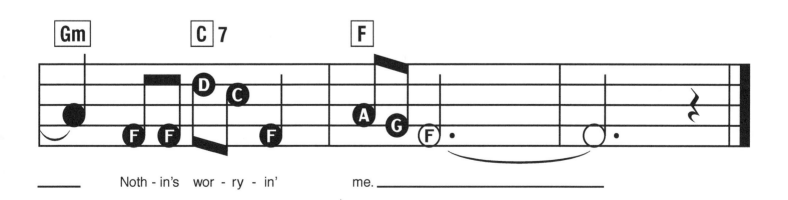

_____   Noth - in's   wor - ry - in'   me. _____

Sunny

Regi-Sound Program: 4
Rhythm: 8-Beat

Words and Music by
Bobby Hebb

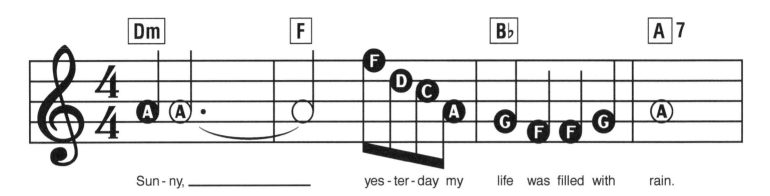

Sun - ny, _____ yes - ter - day my life was filled with rain.

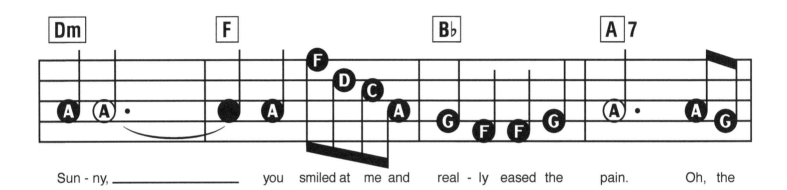

Sun - ny, _____ you smiled at me and real - ly eased the pain. Oh, the

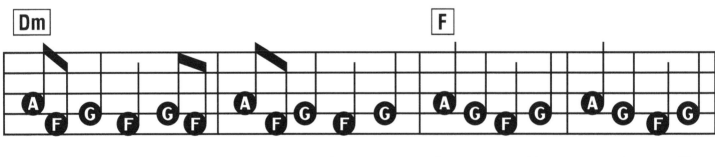

dark days are gone and the bright days are here. My Sun - ny one shines so sin - cere. Oh,

Regi-Sound
Program: 8
(2nd time)

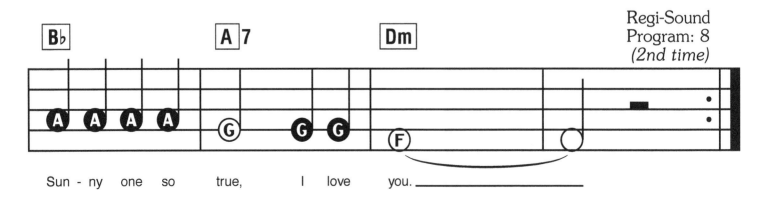

Sun - ny one so true, I love you. _____

Copyright © 1966 Portable Music Company, Inc.
Copyright Renewed
All Rights Administered by BMG Rights Management (US) LLC
All Rights Reserved   Used by Permission

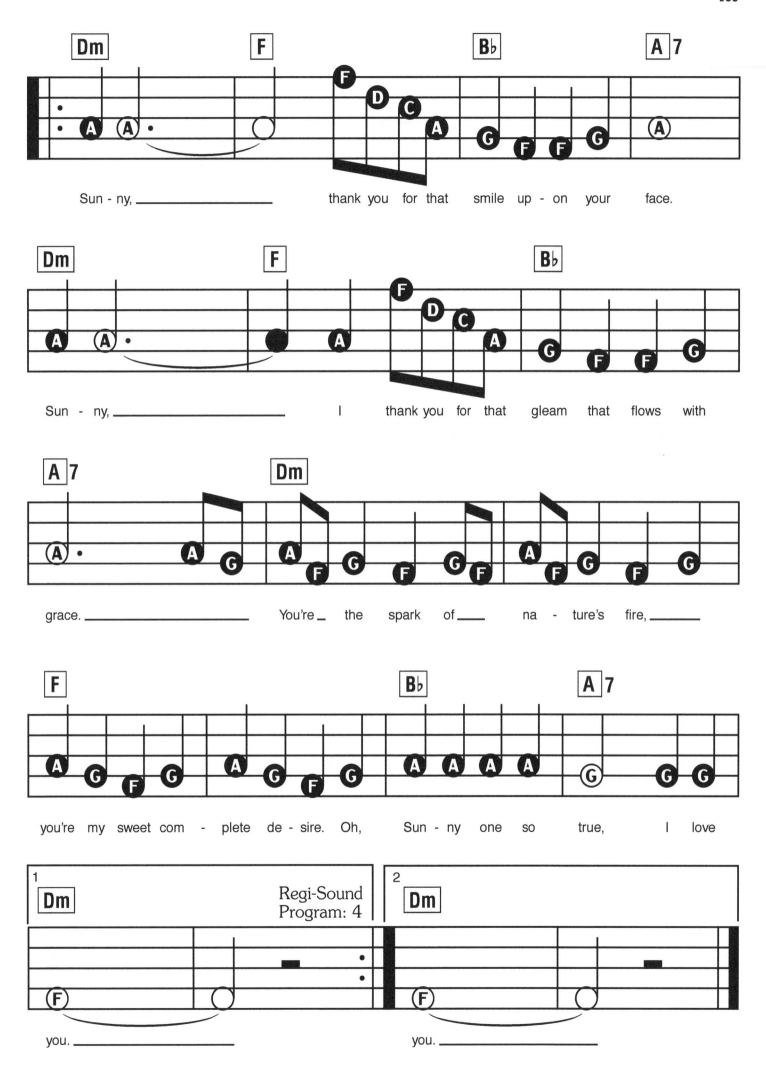

Moon River
from the Paramount Picture BREAKFAST AT TIFFANY'S

Regi-Sound Program: 8
Rhythm: Waltz

Words by Johnny Mercer
Music by Henry Mancini

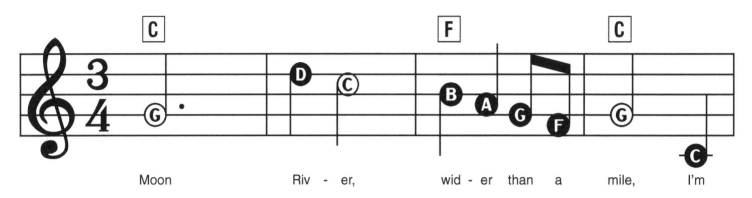

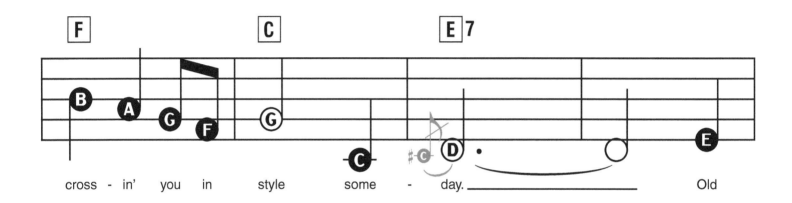

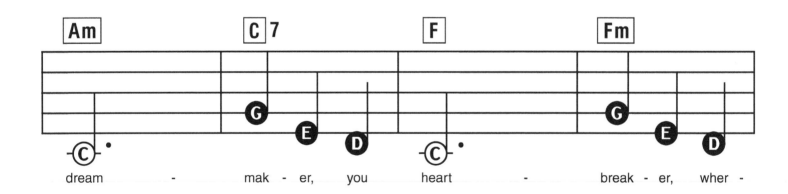

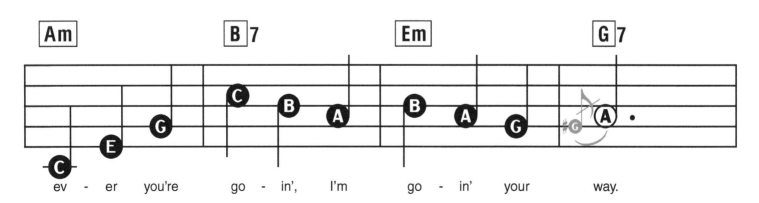

Copyright © 1961 Sony/ATV Music Publishing LLC
Copyright Renewed
All Rights Administered by Sony/ATV Music Publishing LLC, 8 Music Square West, Nashville, TN 37203
International Copyright Secured All Rights Reserved

111

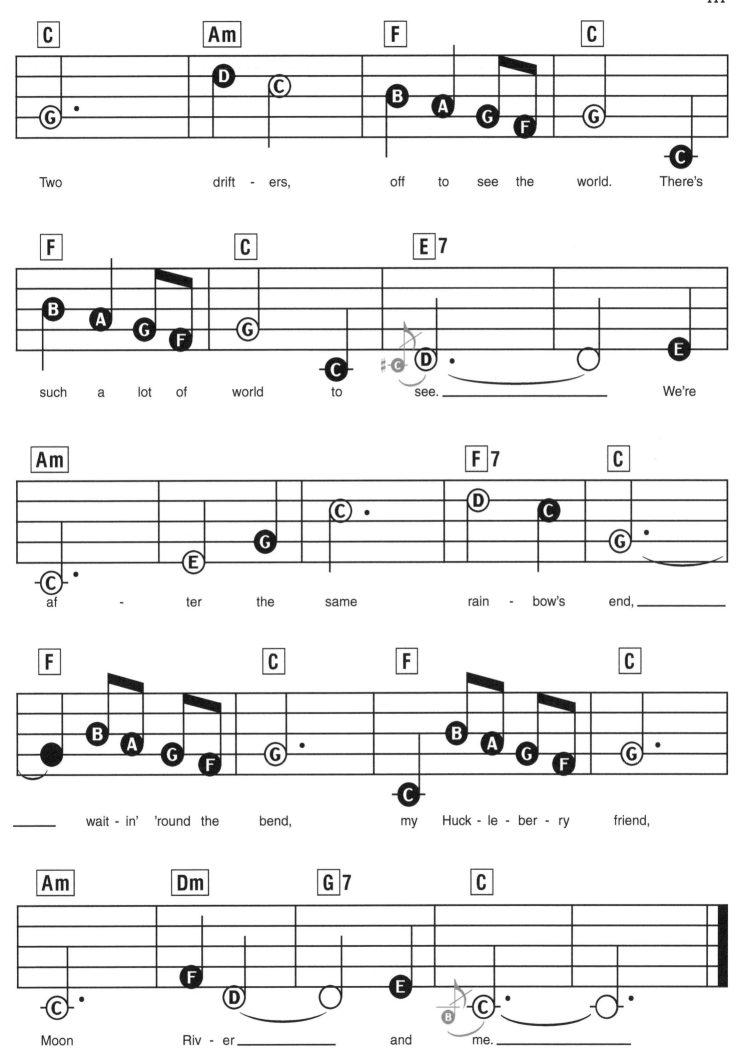

Ramblin' Rose

Regi-Sound Program: 2
Rhythm: Fox Trot

Words and Music by Noel Sherman
and Joe Sherman

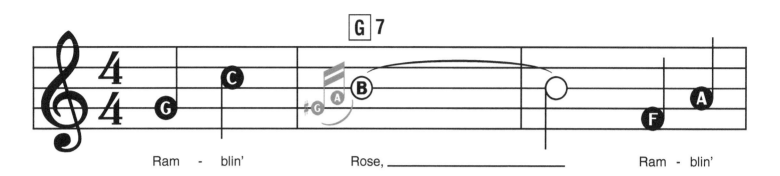

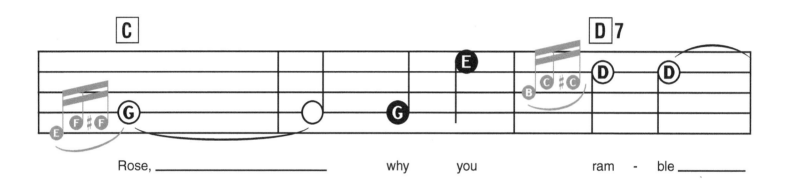

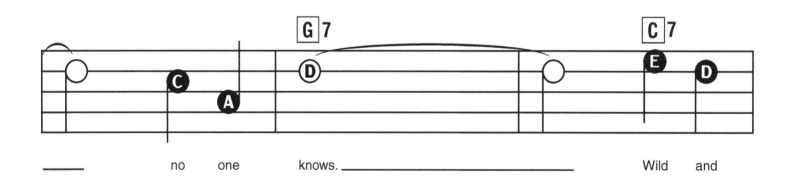

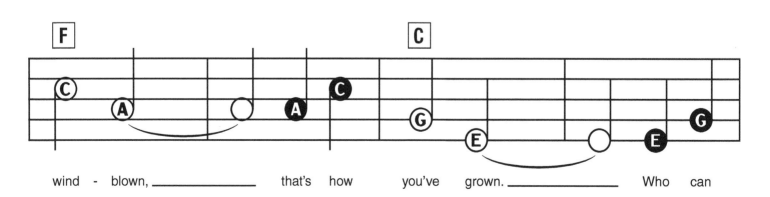

Copyright © 1962 Sony/ATV Music Publishing LLC and Erasmus Music, Inc.
Copyright Renewed
All Rights Administered by Sony/ATV Music Publishing LLC,
  8 Music Square West, Nashville, TN 37203
International Copyright Secured All Rights Reserved

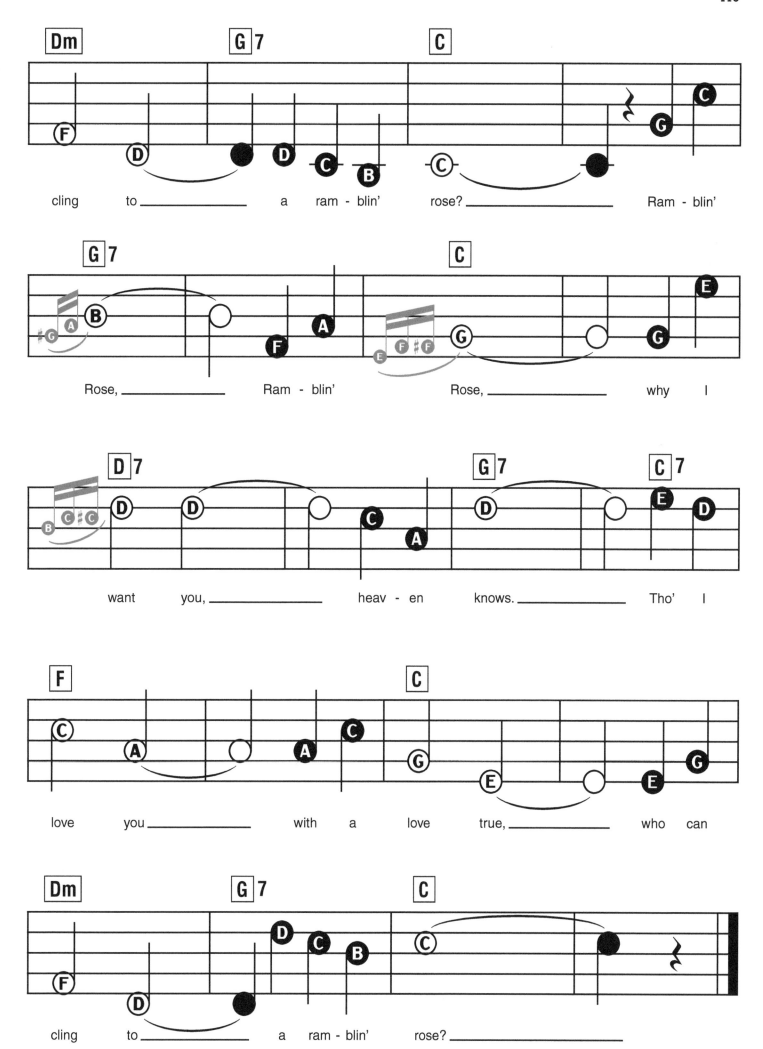

Beauty and the Beast
from Walt Disney's BEAUTY AND THE BEAST

Regi-Sound Program: 1
Rhythm: 8-Beat or Ballad

Lyrics by Howard Ashman
Music by Alan Menken

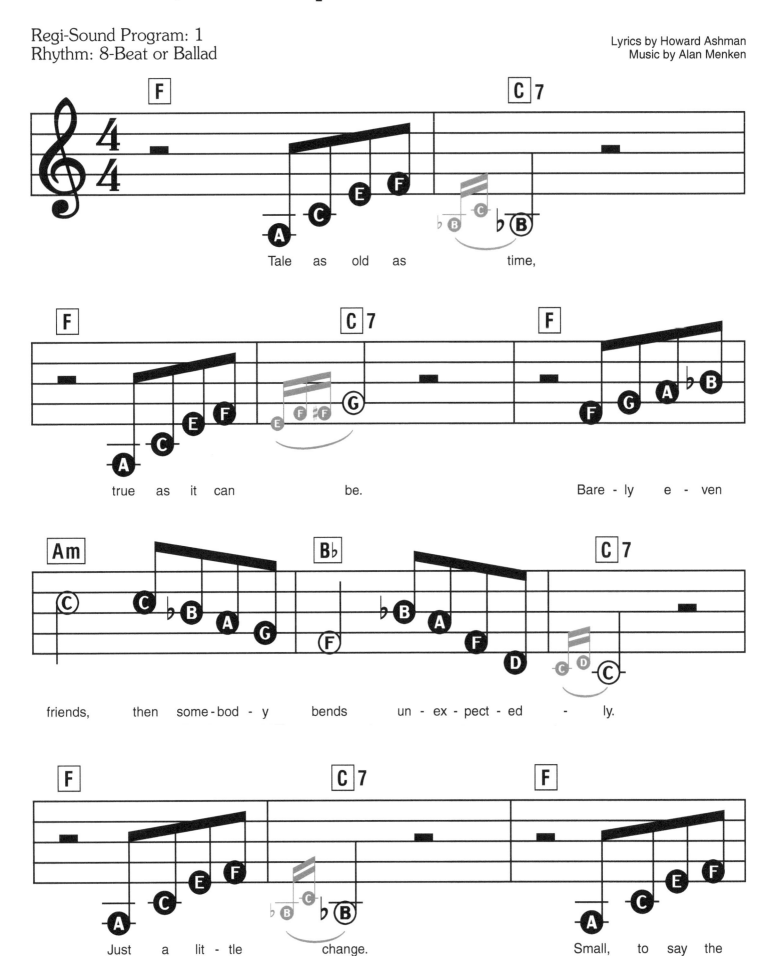

© 1991 Walt Disney Music Company and Wonderland Music Company, Inc.
All Rights Reserved   Used by Permission

116

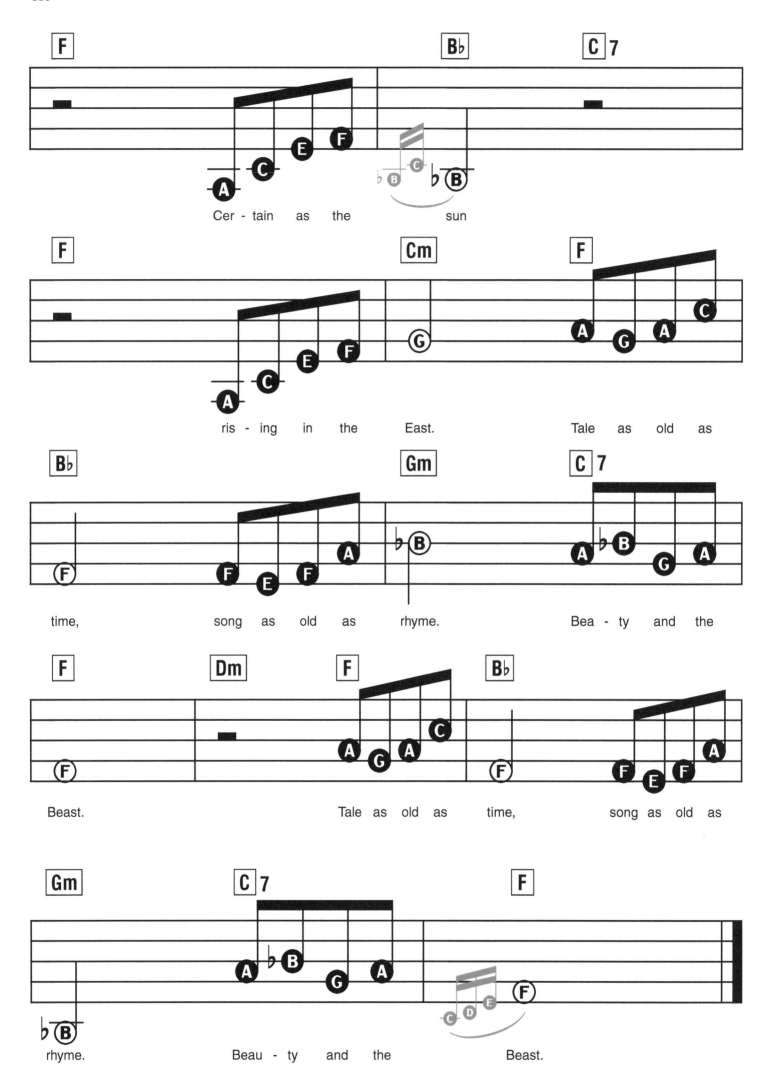

Candle in the Wind

Regi-Sound Program: 8
Rhythm: Ballad

Words and Music by Elton John
and Bernie Taupin

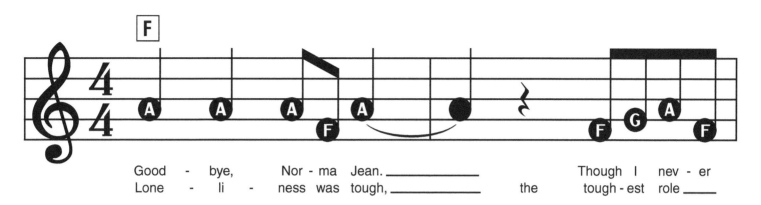

Good - bye, Nor - ma Jean. _____ Though I nev - er
Lone - li - ness was tough, _____ the tough - est role _____

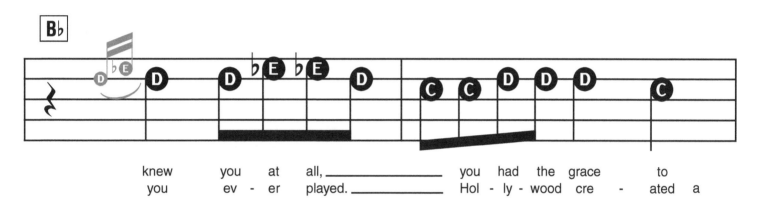

knew you at all, _____ you had the grace to
you ev - er played. _____ Hol - ly - wood cre - ated a

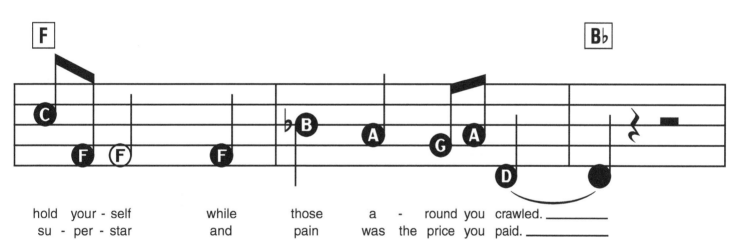

hold your - self while those a - round you crawled. _____
su - per - star and pain was the price you paid. _____

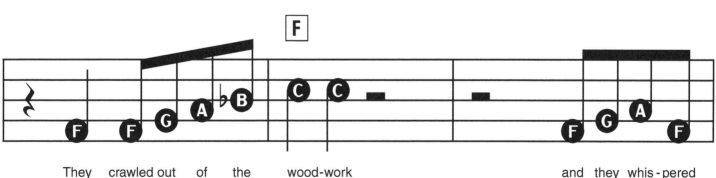

They crawled out of the wood - work and they whis - pered
And e - ven when you died, _____ oh, the press

Copyright © 1973 UNIVERSAL/DICK JAMES MUSIC LTD.
Copyright Renewed
All Rights in the United States and Canada Controlled and Administered by
UNIVERSAL-SONGS OF POLYGRAM INTERNATIONAL, INC.
All Rights Reserved   Used by Permission

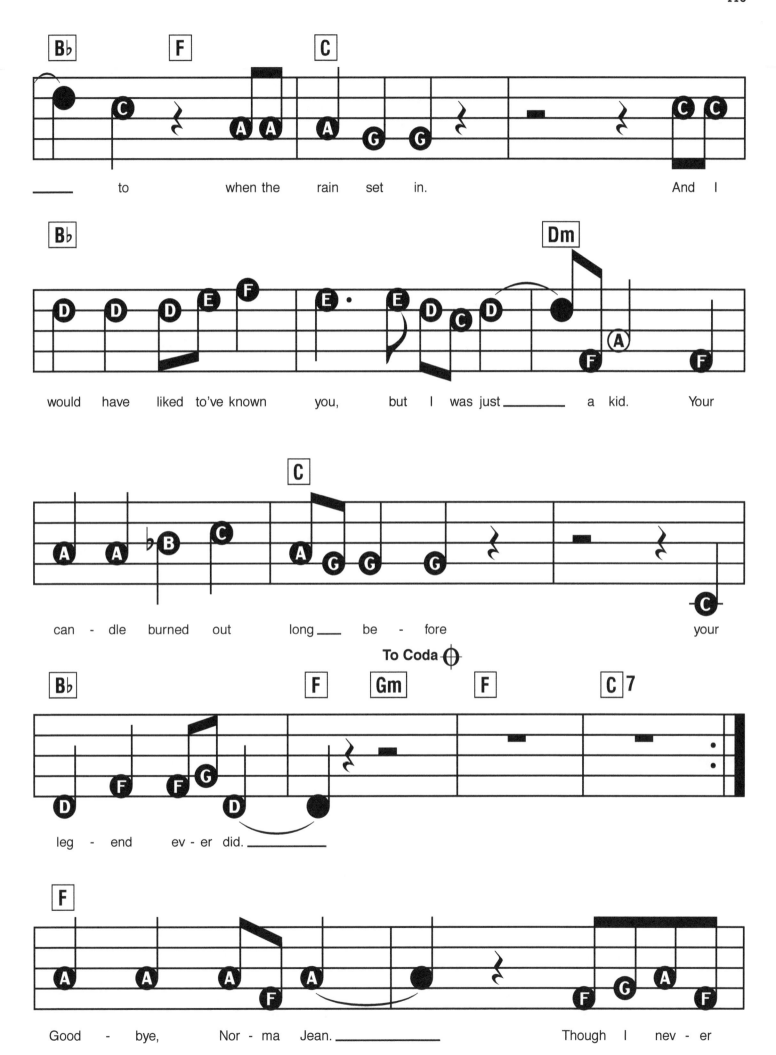

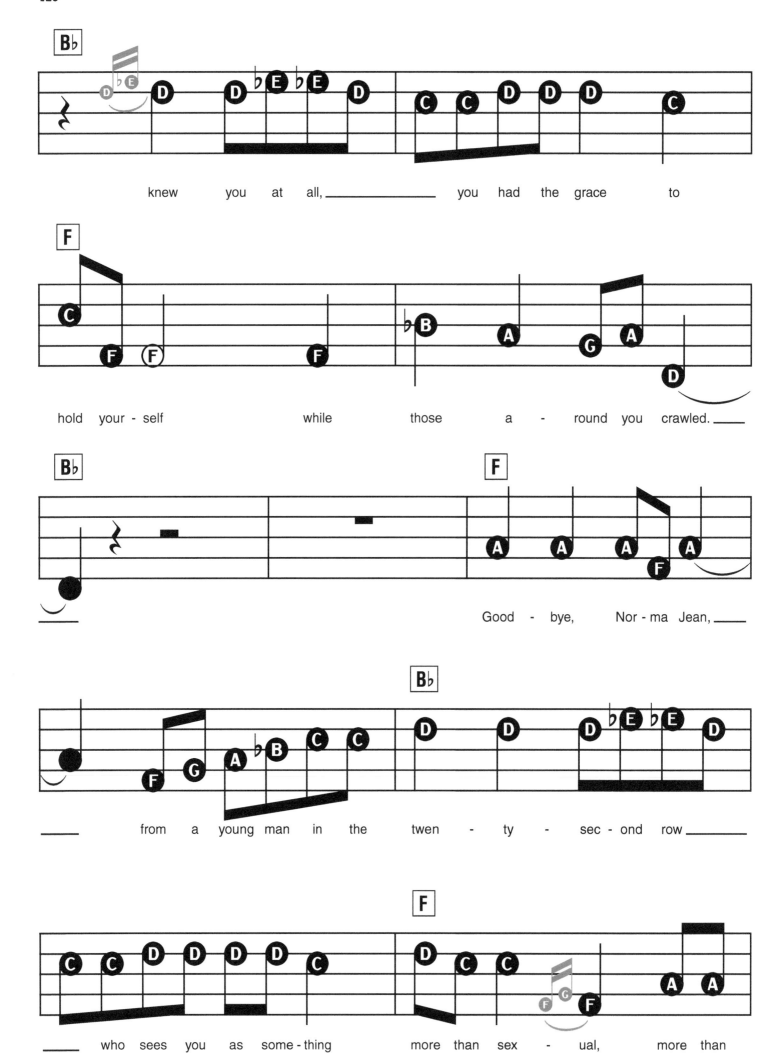

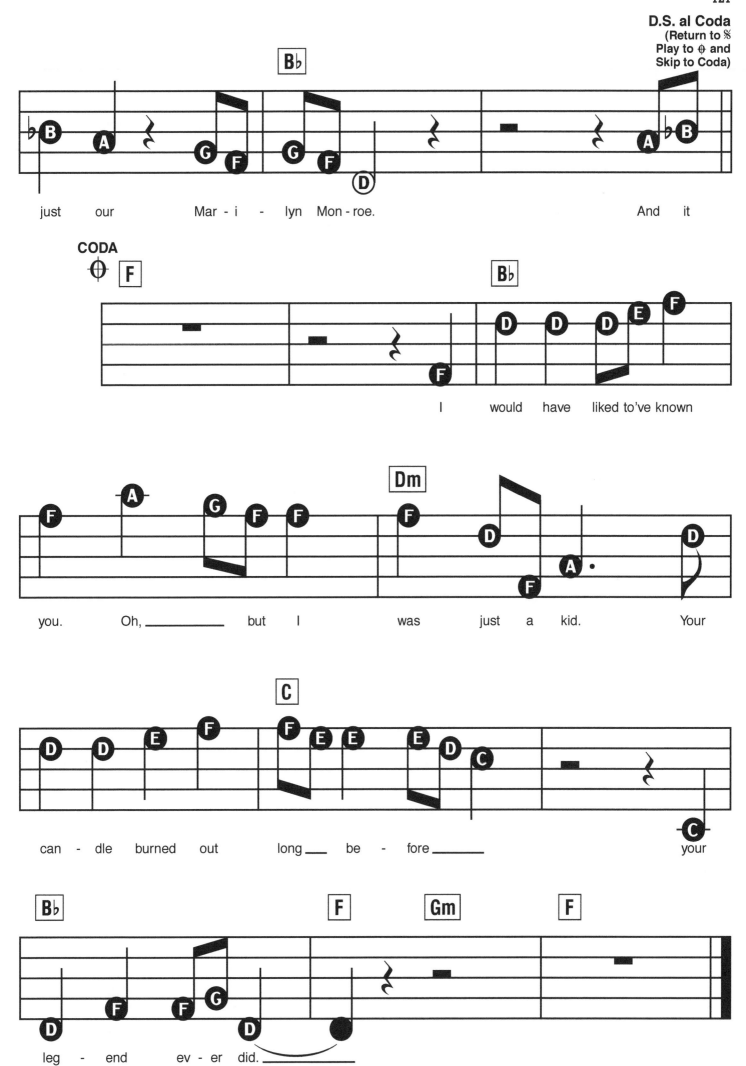

D.S. al Coda
(Return to %
Play to ⊕ and
Skip to Coda)

A Hard Day's Night

Regi-Sound Program: 7
Rhythm: 8-Beat or Rock

Words and Music by John Lennon
and Paul McCartney

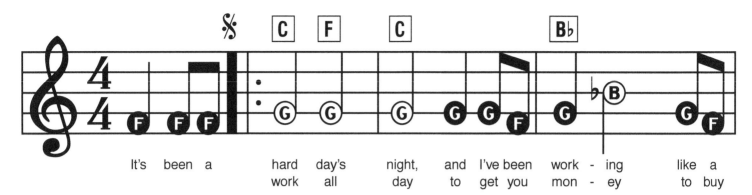

It's been a hard day's night, and I've been work - ing like a
work all day to get you mon - ey to buy

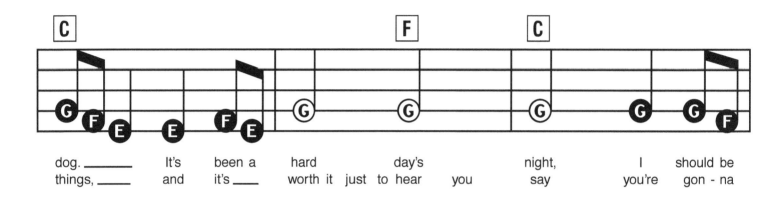

dog. _____ It's been a hard day's night, I should be
things, _____ and it's _____ worth it just to hear you say you're gon - na

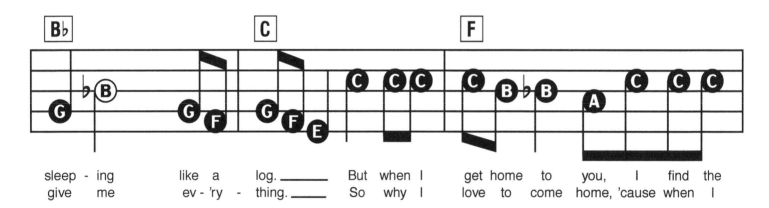

sleep - ing like a log. _____ But when I get home to you, I find the
give me ev - 'ry - thing. _____ So why I love to come home, 'cause when I

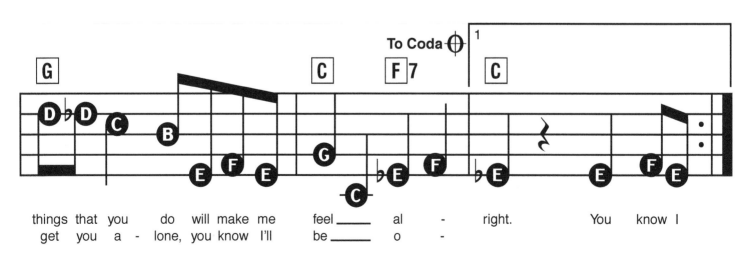

things that you do will make me feel _____ al - right. You know I
get you a - lone, you know I'll be _____ o -

Copyright © 1964 Sony/ATV Music Publishing LLC
Copyright Renewed
All Rights Administered by Sony/ATV Music Publishing LLC,
   8 Music Square West, Nashville, TN 37203
International Copyright Secured   All Rights Reserved

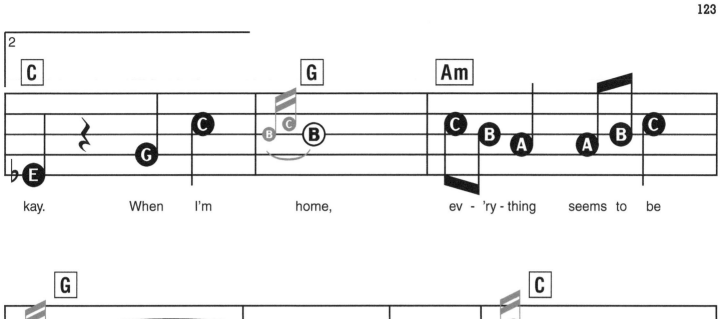

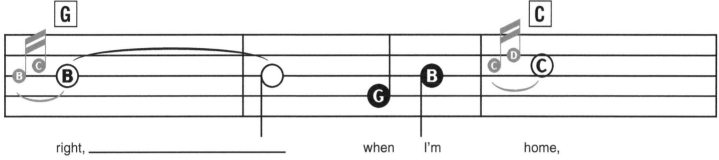

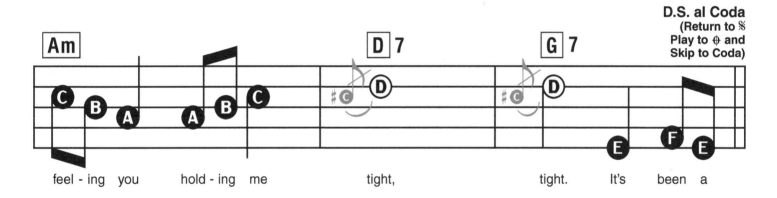

D.S. al Coda
(Return to 𝄋
Play to ⊕ and
Skip to Coda)

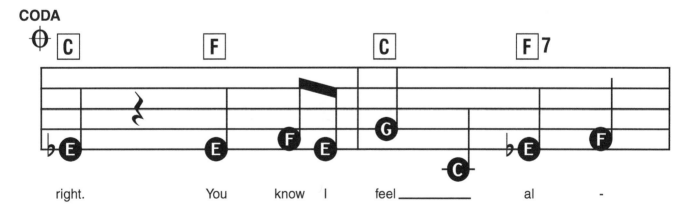

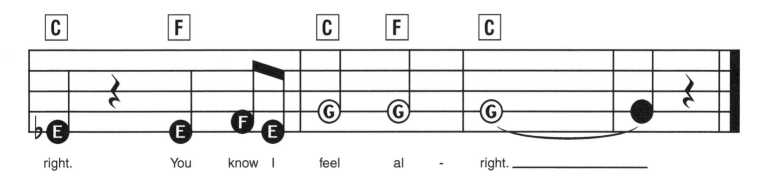

Hey Jude

Regi-Sound Program: 4
Rhythm: 8-Beat or Rock

Words and Music by John Lennon
and Paul McCartney

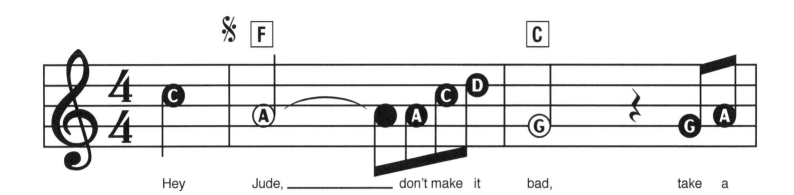

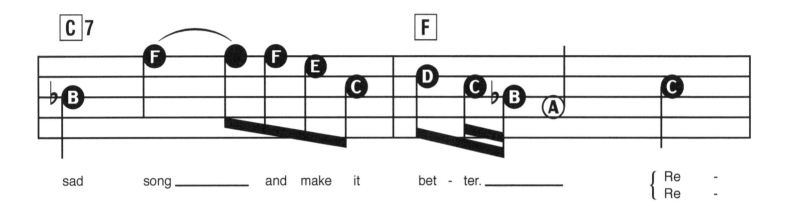

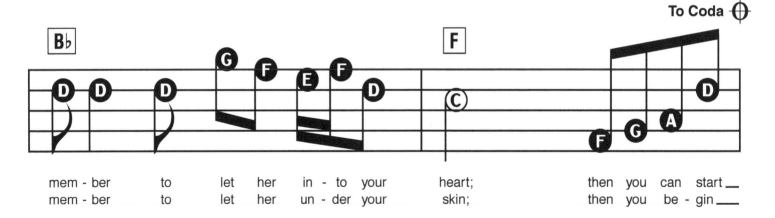

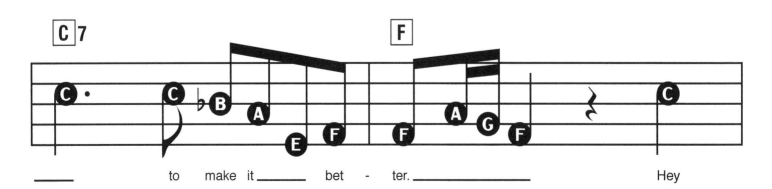

Copyright © 1968 Sony/ATV Music Publishing LLC
Copyright Renewed
All Rights Administered by Sony/ATV Music Publishing LLC, 8 Music Square West, Nashville, TN 37203
International Copyright Secured   All Rights Reserved

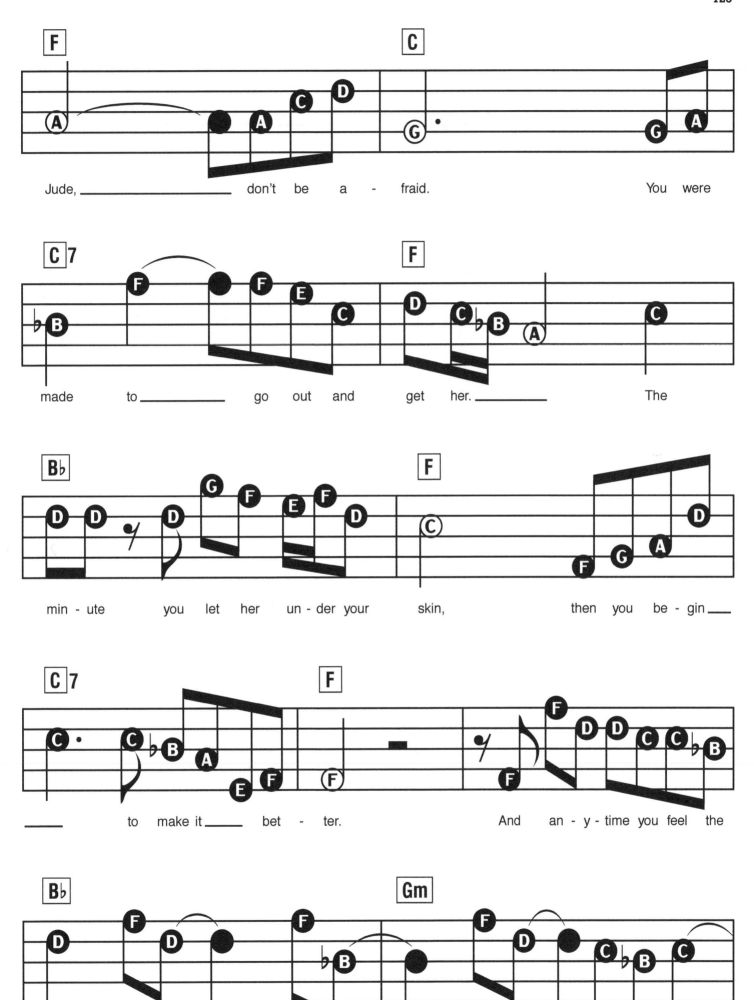

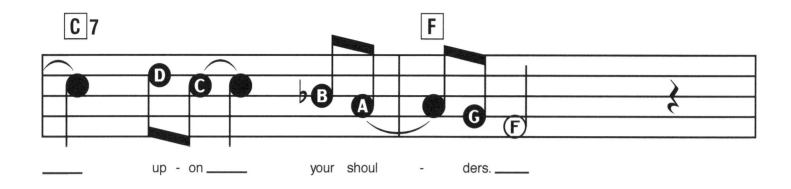

up - on _____ your shoul - ders. _____

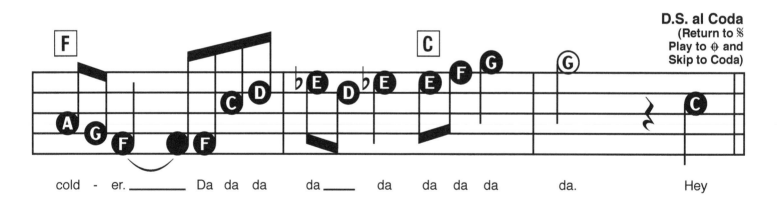

For well you know that it's a fool who plays it cool _____

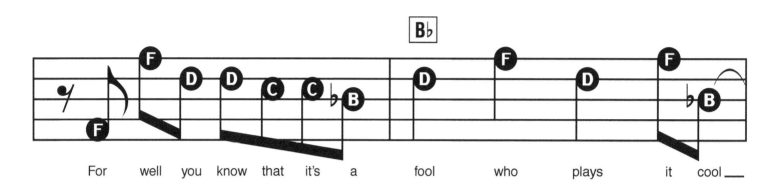

_____ by mak - ing his world _____ a lit - tle

D.S. al Coda
(Return to 𝄋
Play to ⊕ and
Skip to Coda)

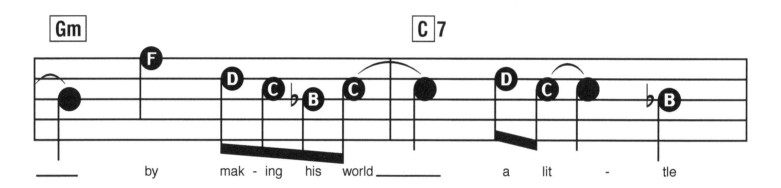

cold - er. _____ Da da da da _____ da da da da da. Hey

CODA

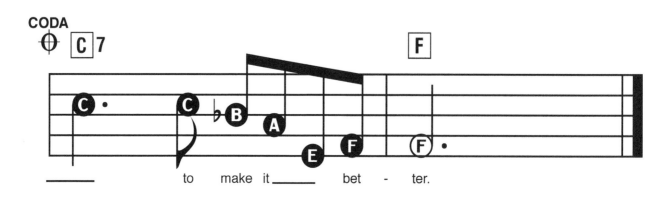

_____ to make it _____ bet - ter.

A Pirate's Life
from Walt Disney's PETER PAN

Regi-Sound Program: 2
Rhythm: 6/8 March

Words by Ed Penner
Music by Oliver Wallace

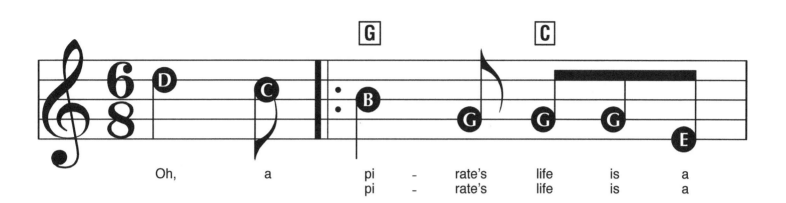

Oh, a pi - rate's life is a
pi - rate's life is a

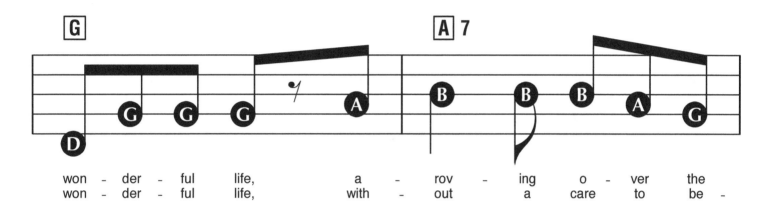

won - der - ful life, a - rov - ing o - ver the
won - der - ful life, with - out a care to be -

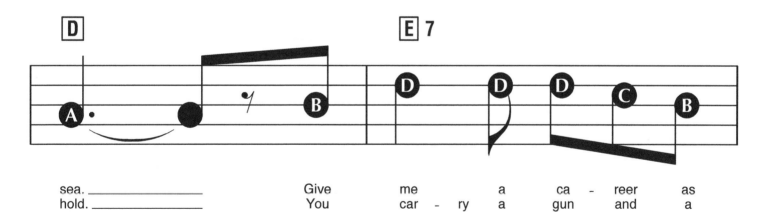

sea. _____ Give me a ca - reer as
hold. _____ You car - ry a gun and a

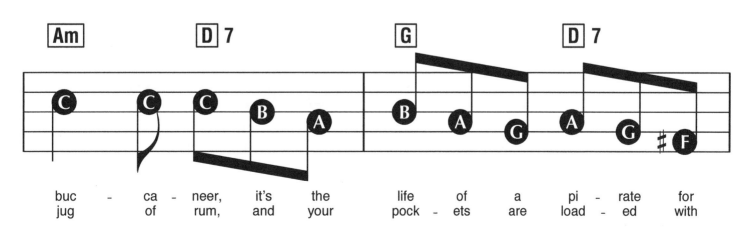

buc - ca - neer, it's the life of a pi - rate for
jug of rum, and your pock - ets are load - ed for with

© 1951 Walt Disney Music Company
Copyright Renewed
All Rights Reserved   Used by Permission

128

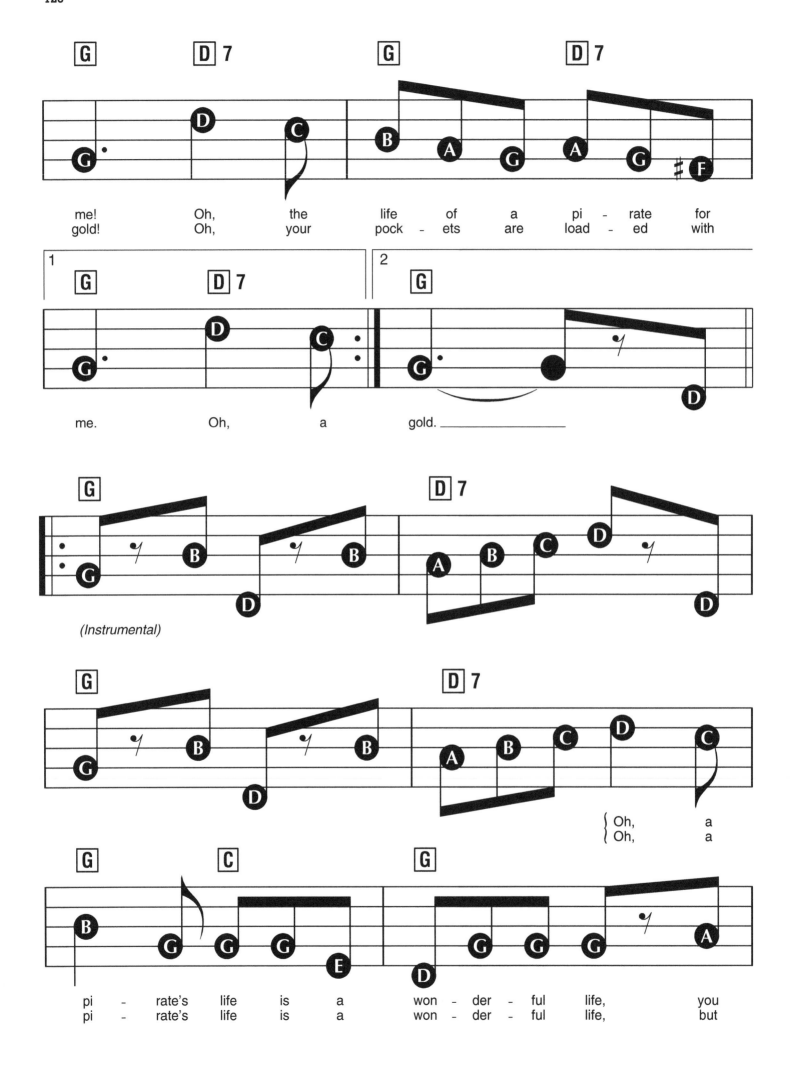

(Instrumental)

me! Oh, the life of a pi - rate for
gold! Oh, your pock - ets are load - ed for with

me. Oh, a
gold. _____

Oh, a
Oh, a

pi - rate's life is a won - der - ful life, you
pi - rate's life is a won - der - ful life, but

Hey, Look Me Over
from WILDCAT

Regi-Sound Program: 7
Rhythm: 6/8 March

Music by Cy Coleman
Lyrics by Carolyn Leigh

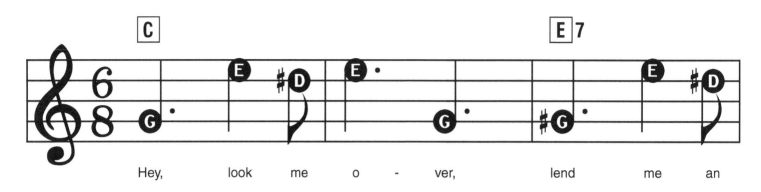

Hey, look me o - ver, lend me an

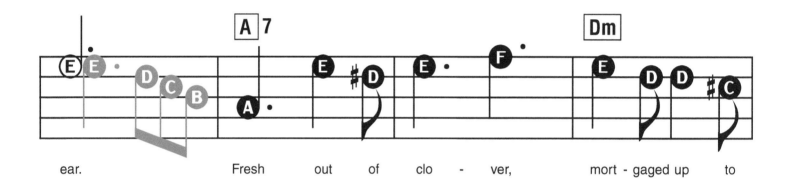

ear. Fresh out of clo - ver, mort - gaged up to

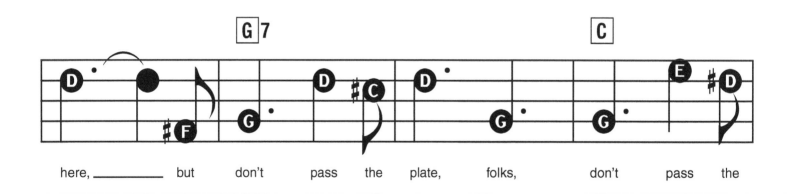

here, _____ but don't pass the plate, folks, don't pass the

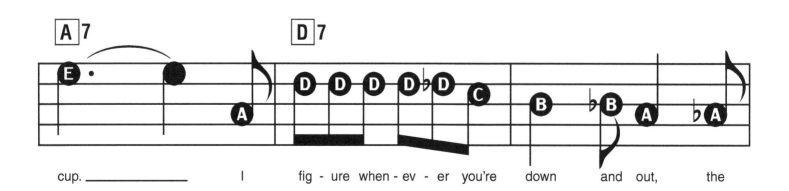

cup. _____ I fig - ure when - ev - er you're down and out, the

Copyright © 1960 Notable Music Company, Inc. and EMI Carwin Music Inc.
Copyright Renewed
All Rights Reserved   Used by Permission

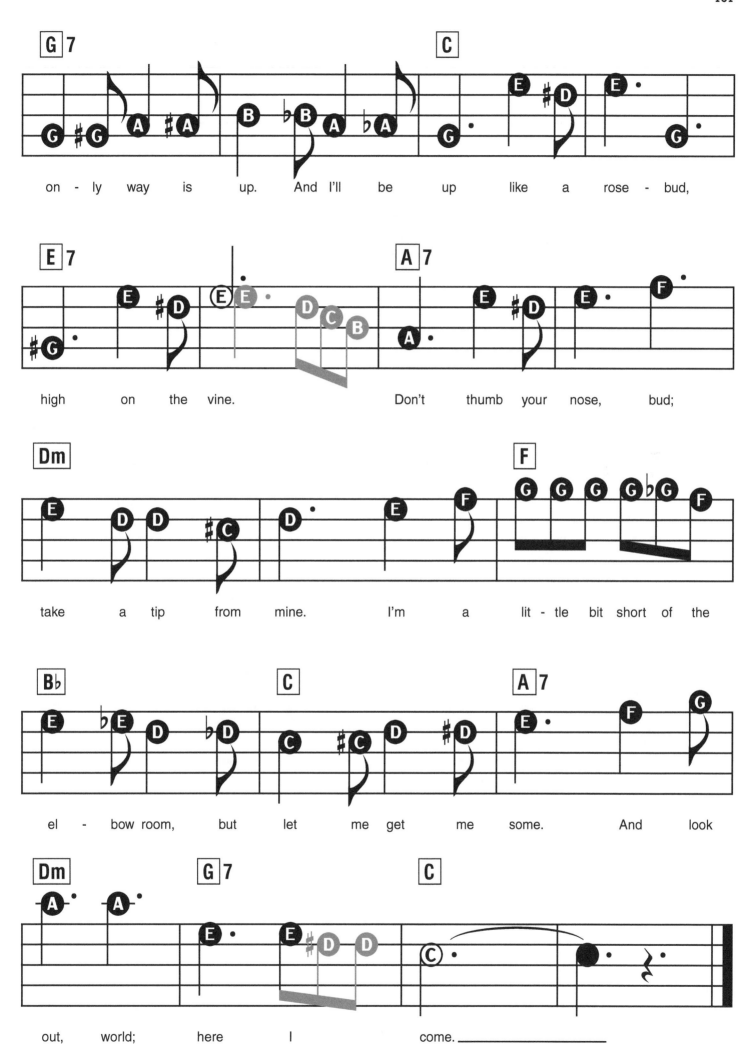

Everything Is Beautiful

Regi-Sound Program: 8
Rhythm: Country Rock

Words and Music by
Ray Stevens

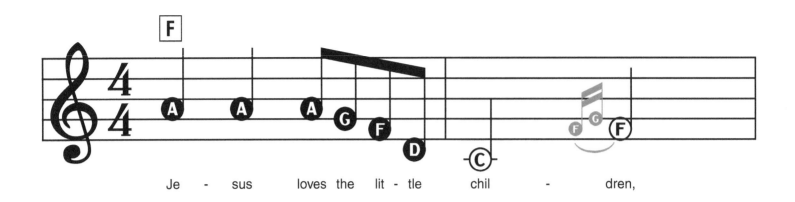

Je - sus loves the lit - tle chil - dren,

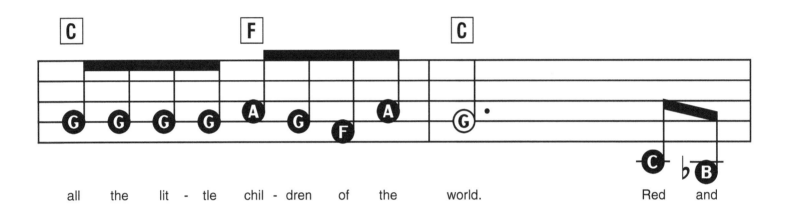

all the lit - tle chil - dren of the world. Red and

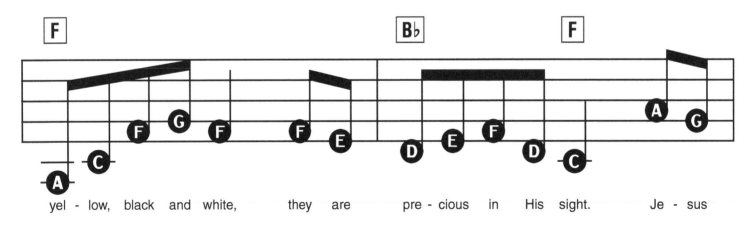

yel - low, black and white, they are pre - cious in His sight. Je - sus

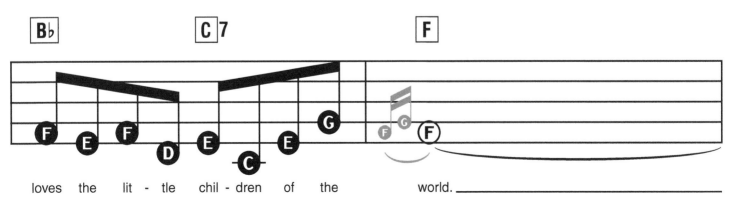

loves the lit - tle chil - dren of the world. _____

© Copyright 1970 (Renewed 1998) Ahab Music Company, Inc. (BMI) (admin. by ClearBox Rights)
All Rights Reserved   Used by Permission

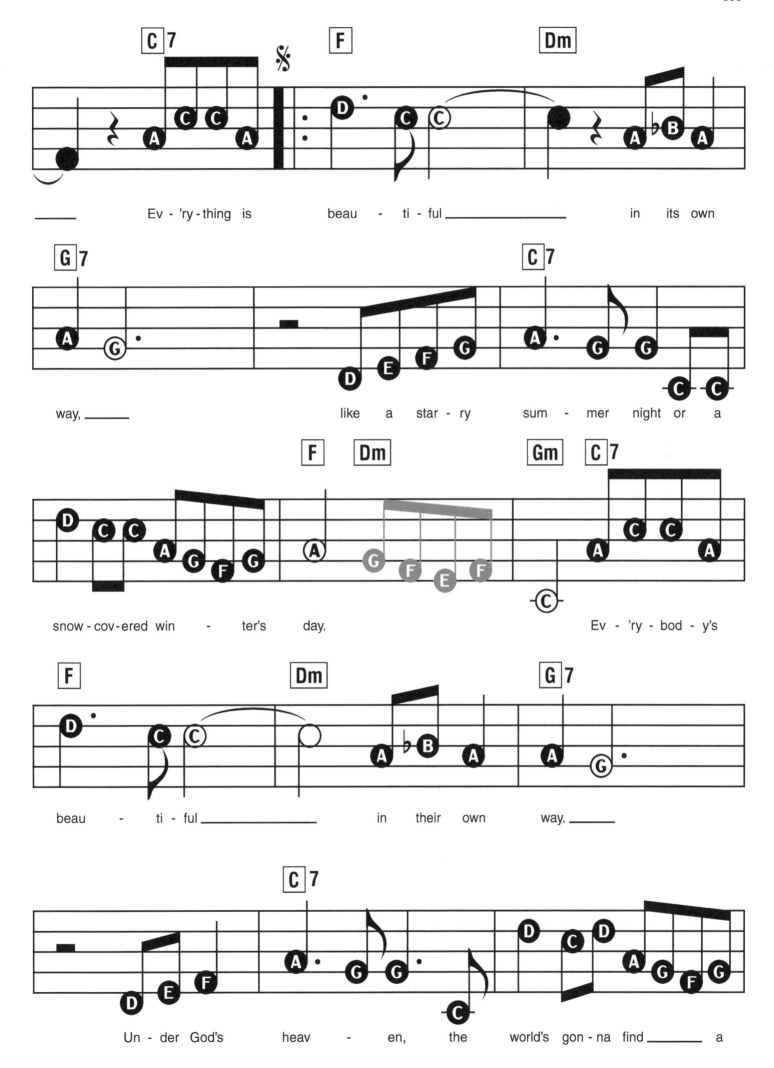

133

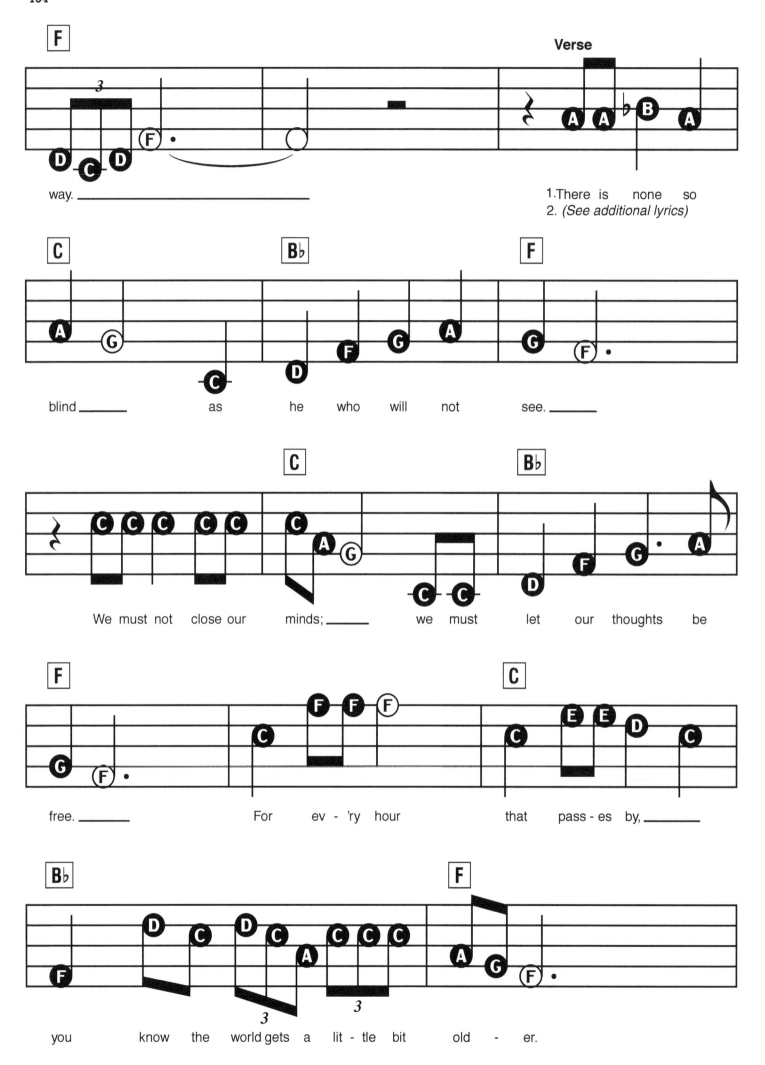

134

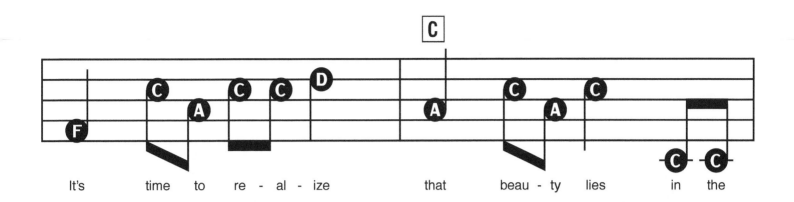

It's   time   to   re - al - ize   that   beau - ty   lies   in   the

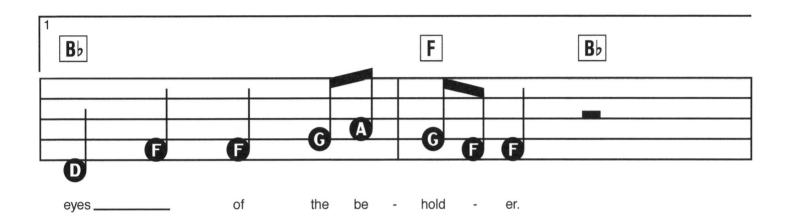

eyes _____   of   the   be - hold - er.

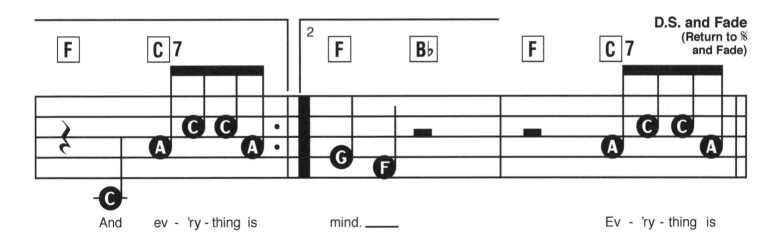

And   ev - 'ry - thing is   mind. ____   Ev - 'ry - thing is

D.S. and Fade
(Return to 𝄋
and Fade)

Additional Lyrics

2. We shouldn't care about the length of his hair or the color of his skin.
Don't worry about what shows from without but the love that lives within.
We're gonna get it all together now and everything's gonna work out fine.
Just take a little time to look on the good side, my friend, and straighten it
out in your mind.

Cab Driver

Regi-Sound Program: 7
Rhythm: Fox Trot

Words and Music by
C. Carson Parks

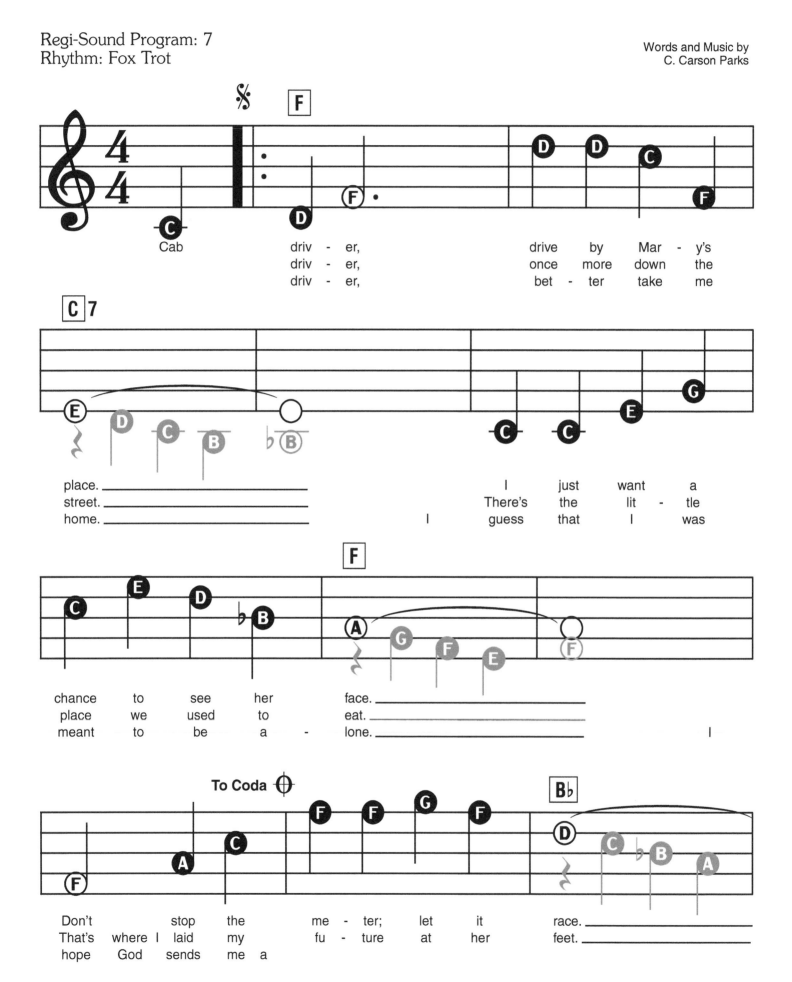

Copyright © 1963 Greenwood Music Co., R.R. #1, Box 496, Waynesville, NC 28786
Copyright Renewed
International Copyright Secured   All Rights Reserved

137

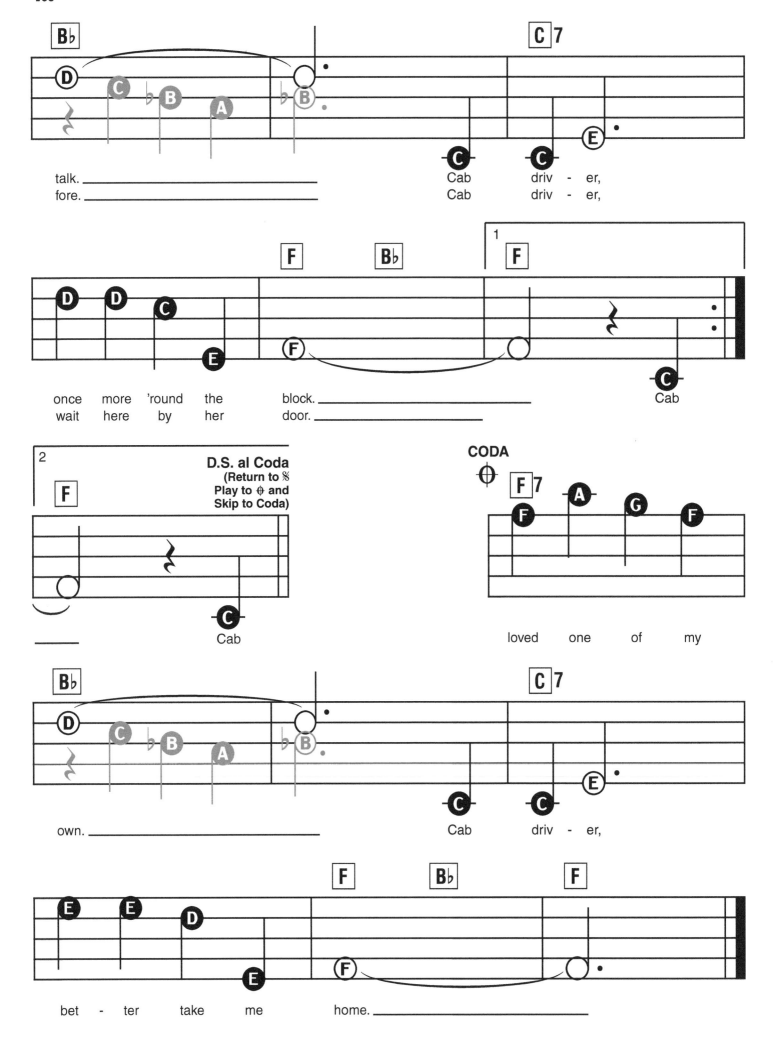

Sweet Caroline

Regi-Sound Program: 2
Rhythm: Fox Trot

Words and Music by
Neil Diamond

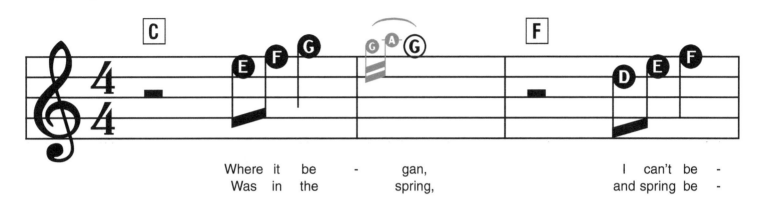

Where it be - gan,   I can't be -
Was in the spring,   and spring be -

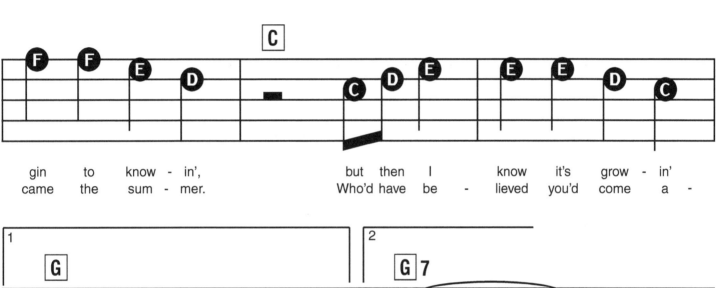

gin to know - in',   but then I know it's grow - in'
came the sum - mer.   Who'd have be - lieved you'd come a -

strong. _____   long? _____

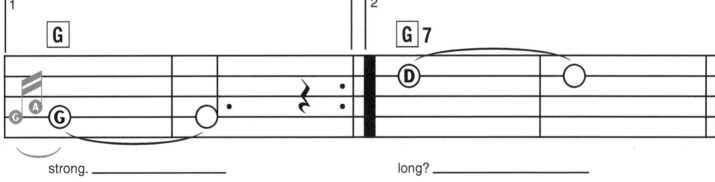

Hands, _____   touch-in' hands, _____   reach-in' out, _____
Warm, _____   touch-in' warm, _____

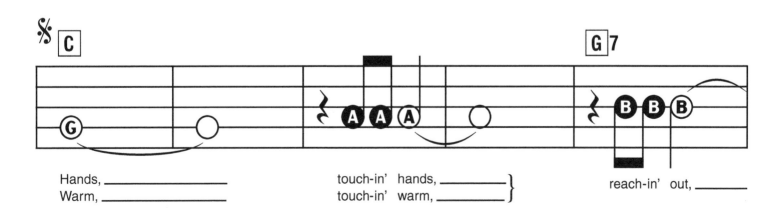

© 1969 (Renewed) STONEBRIDGE MUSIC
All Rights Reserved

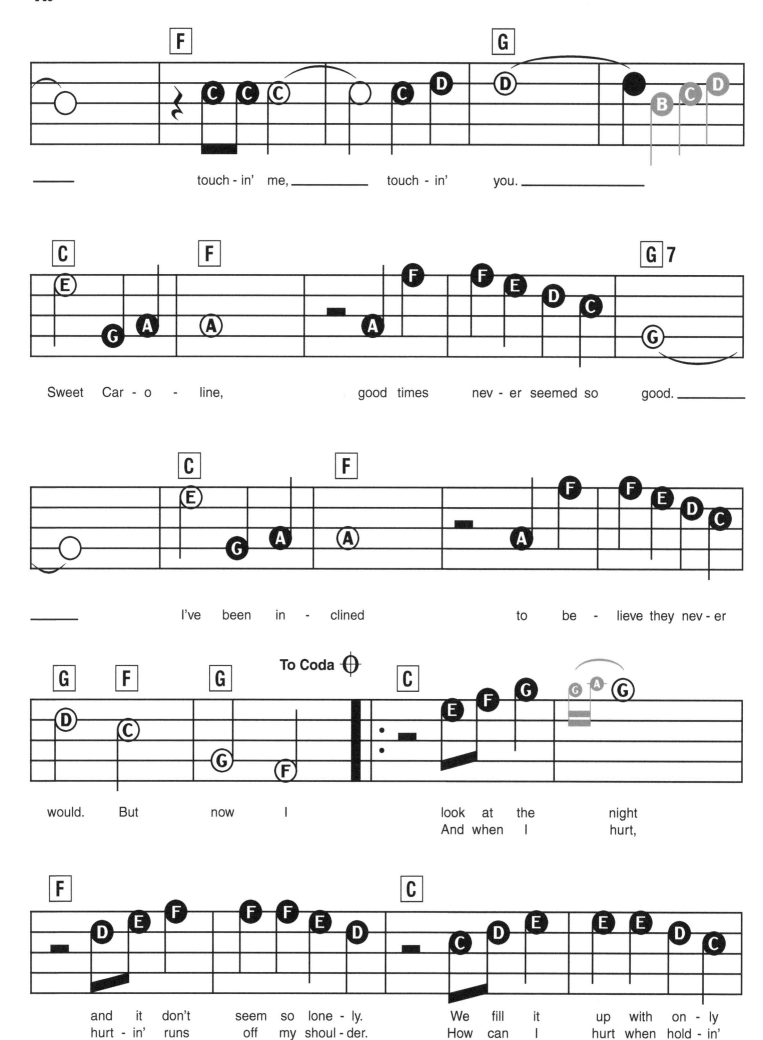

touch - in' me, _____ touch - in' you. _____

Sweet Car - o - line, good times nev - er seemed so good. _____

_____ I've been in - clined to be - lieve they nev - er

would. But now I look at the night
And when I hurt,

and it don't seem so lone - ly. We fill it up with on - ly
hurt - in' runs off my shoul - der. How can I hurt when hold - in'

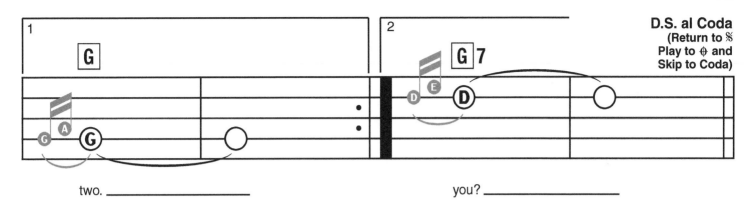

D.S. al Coda
(Return to ⅌
Play to ⊕ and
Skip to Coda)

two. _____   you? _____

CODA

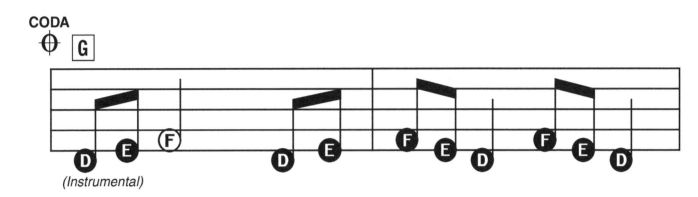

(Instrumental)

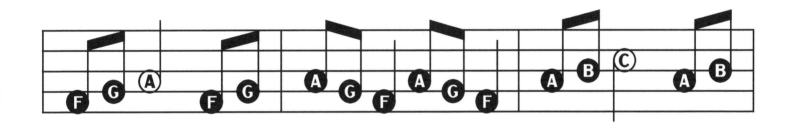

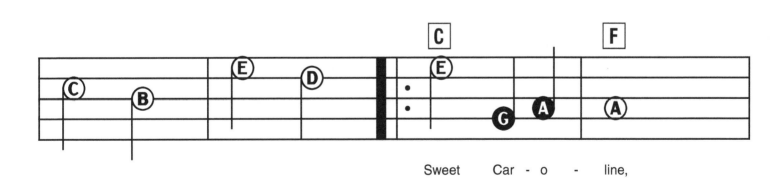

Sweet   Car - o - line,

Repeat and Fade

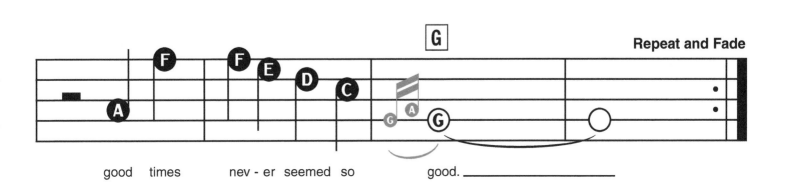

good   times   nev - er   seemed so   good. _____

Tennessee Waltz

Regi-Sound Program: 10
Rhythm: Waltz

Words and Music by Redd Stewart
and Pee Wee King

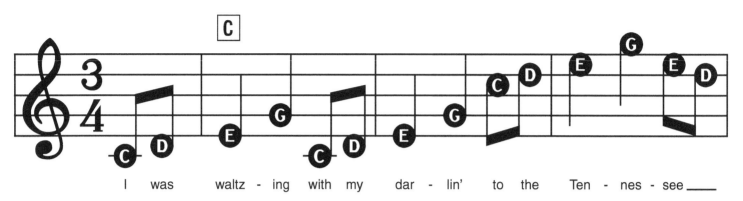

I was waltz - ing with my dar - lin' to the Ten - nes - see ____

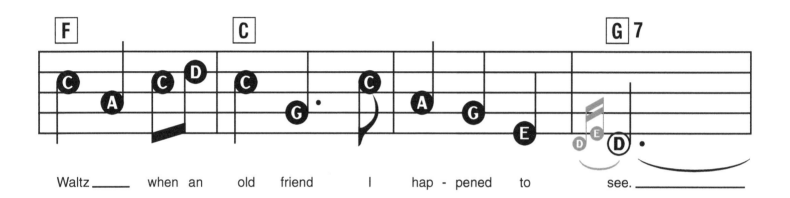

Waltz ____ when an old friend I hap - pened to see. ____

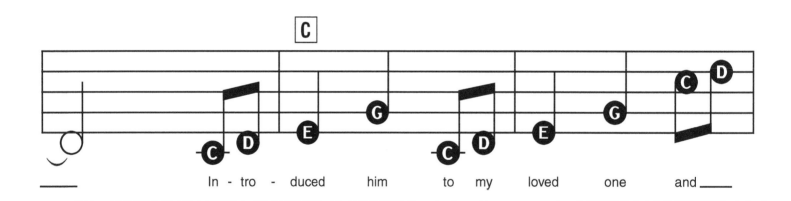

____ In - tro - duced him to my loved one and ____

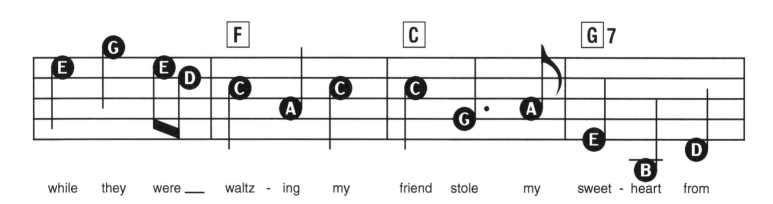

while they were ____ waltz - ing my friend stole my sweet - heart from

Copyright © 1948 Sony/ATV Music Publishing LLC
Copyright Renewed
All Rights Administered by Sony/ATV Music Publishing LLC,
  8 Music Square West, Nashville, TN 37203
International Copyright Secured All Rights Reserved

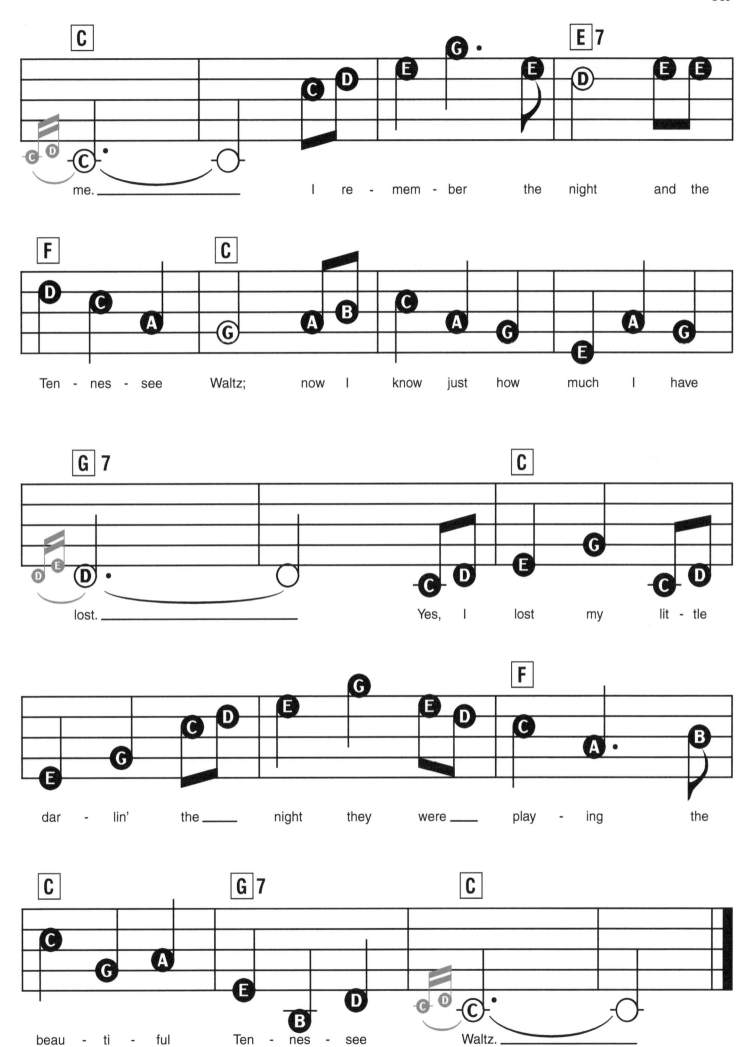

FOR ORGANS, PIANOS & ELECTRONIC KEYBOARDS

E-Z PLAY® TODAY PUBLICATIONS

The E-Z Play® Today songbook series is the shortest distance between beginning music and playing fun!
Check out this list of highlights and visit balleonard.com for a complete listing of all volumes and songlists.

HAL•LEONARD®

Prices, contents and availability
subject to change without notice

0421
330